# Teens and Privacy

# Other Books in the Current Controversies Series

Biodiversity

Blogs

Capital Punishment

Darfur

Disaster Response

Drug Trafficking

Espionage and Intelligence

Factory Farming

Global Warming

Human Trafficking

Immigration

Online Social Networking

Poverty and Homelessness

Prisons

Racism

Resitant Infections

The U.S. Economy

The World Economy

Urban Sprawl

Violence Against Women

# Teens and Privacy

*Noël Merino, Book Editor*

**GREENHAVEN PRESS**
*A part of Gale, Cengage Learning*

GALE
CENGAGE Learning

Detroit • New York • San Francisco • New Haven, Conn • Waterville, Maine • London

Christine Nasso, *Publisher*
Elizabeth Des Chenes, *Managing Editor*

*For more information, contact:*
Greenhaven Press
27500 Drake Rd.
Farmington Hills, MI 48331-3535
Or you can visit our Internet site at gale.cengage.com

For product information and technology assistance, contact us at

Gale Customer Support, 1-800-877-4253
For permission to use material from this text or product, submit all requests online at www.cengage.com/permissions

Further permissions questions can be emailed to permissionrequest@cengage.com

Articles In Greenhaven Press anthologies are often edited for length to meet page requirements. In addition, original titles of these works are changed to clearly present the main thesis and to explicitly indicate the author's opinion. Every effort is made to ensure that Greenhaven Press accurately reflects the original intent of the authors. Every effort has been made to trace the owners of copyrighted material.

Cover image copyright © Tetra Images/Corbis.

**LIBRARY OF CONGRESS CATALOGING-IN-PUBLICATION DATA**

Teens and Privacy / Noël Merino, book editor.
  p. cm. -- (Current controversies)
  Includes bibliographical references and index.
  ISBN 978-0-7377-5133-8 (hbk.) -- ISBN 978-0-7377-5134-5 (pbk.)
  1. Teenagers. 2. Privacy, Right of. 3. Parent and teenager. I. Merino, Noël.
  HQ799.15.T445 2011
  323.44'80835--dc22
                                                                    2010042275

Printed in the United States of America
2 3 4 5 6 7 15 14 13 12 11

# Contents

Foreword      **11**

Introduction      **14**

## Chapter 1: Do Teens Have a Right to Privacy?

Chapter Preface      **18**

### Yes: Teens Have a Right to Privacy

Teens Have a Right to Privacy from Parents      **20**
*Melanie Barwick*

Teens have a need for privacy, and parents should respect that need as much as possible or risk the negative consequences.

Children Need Some Places Where They Have Privacy from Adults      **26**
*Michael Thompson*

Having private time away from adults is an important part of growing up and should be allowed within reason.

Teens Should Have a Right to Privacy That Is Earned      **29**
*Kelly Weber*

Privacy is very important for teenagers and, as long they remain trustworthy, their right to privacy should be respected.

### No: Teens Do Not Have a Right to Privacy

Teens Do Not Have a Right to Privacy from Parents      **32**
*Lindsay Ferrier*

It is a parent's job to monitor children at all times, even if that means violating privacy.

To Be a Good Parent, It Is Necessary to Invade Teen Privacy      **35**
Chronicle

Parents have the right and the responsibility to invade the privacy of their children in order to protect them.

# Chapter 2: Should Teens Have Privacy in Receiving Medical Care?

Overview: Minors and Privacy in      40
Medical Care

*Guttmacher Institute*

The laws regarding the ability of minors to consent to sexual and reproductive health care and the ability of parents to make health care decisions for their children vary by state.

## Yes: Teens Should Have Privacy in Receiving Medical Care

Confidential Health Care for Teens      43
Is Good Policy

*Scott J. Spear and Abigail English*

There is significant consensus about the important role confidential medical care plays in furthering adolescent health.

Teens Should Be Allowed an Abortion      51
Without Parental Consent

*Kate Michelman*

State parental involvement laws that mandate parental consent for abortion put teens at risk and deny the realities of teen communication.

Contraceptives Should Be Available to Teens      56
Without Parental Consent

*Center for Reproductive Rights*

Restricting teens' access to contraception by requiring parental consent or notification damages their health and violates their constitutional right to privacy.

Mandatory Reporting Laws Violate      61
the Privacy Rights of Minors

*Sherry F. Colb*

Applying mandatory reporting laws to teenage sex is an overbroad policy that threatens teens' well-being and their privacy rights.

**No: Teens Should Not Have Privacy
in Receiving Medical Care**

Parents Have the Right to Oversee Their                68
Children's Health Care

> *Daniel Patrick Moloney*

> The health care system needs to be reformed in such a
> way to respect parents' rights to make health care deci-
> sions for their children.

Parents Have a Right to Know About                     80
Teen Abortion

> *Mailee R. Smith*

> Parental involvement laws requiring notification when a
> minor seeks abortion are necessary to protect the minor's
> health and parental rights.

Contraceptives Should Not Be Available to              84
Young Teens Without Parental Consent

> *Patriot Ledger*

> Allowing teens in middle school to have access to birth
> control without the consent of a parent abdicates paren-
> tal responsibility and sends the wrong message.

# Chapter 3: Should Teens Have Privacy Rights Respected at School?

Overview: Teen Privacy Rights and Drug                 88
Testing at School

> *Students for Sensible Drug Policy*

> Drug testing students is ineffective, harmful, expensive,
> invasive, and may conflict with state legal guarantees of
> student privacy.

**Yes: Teens Should Have Privacy Rights
Respected at School**

Students Have Rights Preventing Schools                92
from Conducting Unwarranted Searches

> *David Souter*

> Although schools may search students when there is a
> reasonable suspicion of danger, searches without justifi-
> cation are unconstitutional.

Schools Should Not Interfere with Student      **101**
Speech off Campus

*Justin Silverman*

Despite recent court decisions and legislation to the contrary, students have a First Amendment right to free speech outside of school without school interference.

**No: Teens Should Not Have Privacy Rights Respected at School**

Random Student Drug Testing Is an      **105**
Important Tool for Drug Prevention

*Student Drug-Testing Institute*

Random student drug testing is one effective tool in preventing teen drug use that, if done confidentially, does not violate students' right to privacy.

Schools Need Broad Authority to Conduct      **114**
Searches of Students

*National School Boards Association and American Association of School Administrators*

School authorities should be given deference in their judgments on the need to search students, especially for legal and illegal drugs.

Schools Can Rightfully Interfere with      **126**
Student Speech off Campus

*John Roberts*

Schools do not violate students' First Amendment rights by limiting speech promoting illegal drug use, both at school and at events away from school.

# Chapter 4: What Are Some Concerns About Teen Privacy and New Technology?

Overview: Children, Privacy, and Online      **139**
Social Networks

*Federal Trade Commission*

There are risks for teens and younger children engaged in online social networking, and parents need to monitor and educate their children about the risks.

Teen Privacy Is Threatened                                    144
by Social Networking
   *Peter Bazalgette*

   The first generation using social networking still cares
   about privacy and needs protection in place to allow for
   privacy rights in the future.

Teen Online Activity Can Harm Future                          149
College Admissions and Employment
   *Nicole Verardi*

   Teens need to be aware that whatever they post online
   will be there forever, possibly hurting their chances of
   getting into college or getting a job.

Teen Sexting Can Have                                         156
Serious Consequences
   *Joshua D. Herman*

   In Illinois and other states, teen sexting is a crime that
   can lead to a teen being charged with child pornography
   and being branded as a sex offender.

The Legal System Is Overly Harsh                              165
Toward Teen Sexting
   *Radley Balko*

   Charging teens with child pornography for sexting is an
   overreaction to the issue and a misuse of the criminal
   justice system.

Organizations to Contact                                      170

Bibliography                                                  174

Index                                                         179

# Foreword

By definition, controversies are "discussions of questions in which opposing opinions clash" (Webster's Twentieth Century Dictionary Unabridged). Few would deny that controversies are a pervasive part of the human condition and exist on virtually every level of human enterprise. Controversies transpire between individuals and among groups, within nations and between nations. Controversies supply the grist necessary for progress by providing challenges and challengers to the status quo. They also create atmospheres where strife and warfare can flourish. A world without controversies would be a peaceful world; but it also would be, by and large, static and prosaic.

## The Series' Purpose

The purpose of the Current Controversies series is to explore many of the social, political, and economic controversies dominating the national and international scenes today. Titles selected for inclusion in the series are highly focused and specific. For example, from the larger category of criminal justice, Current Controversies deals with specific topics such as police brutality, gun control, white collar crime, and others. The debates in Current Controversies also are presented in a useful, timeless fashion. Articles and book excerpts included in each title are selected if they contribute valuable, long-range ideas to the overall debate. And wherever possible, current information is enhanced with historical documents and other relevant materials. Thus, while individual titles are current in focus, every effort is made to ensure that they will not become quickly outdated. Books in the Current Controversies series will remain important resources for librarians, teachers, and students for many years.

In addition to keeping the titles focused and specific, great care is taken in the editorial format of each book in the series. Book introductions and chapter prefaces are offered to provide background material for readers. Chapters are organized around several key questions that are answered with diverse opinions representing all points on the political spectrum. Materials in each chapter include opinions in which authors clearly disagree as well as alternative opinions in which authors may agree on a broader issue but disagree on the possible solutions. In this way, the content of each volume in Current Controversies mirrors the mosaic of opinions encountered in society. Readers will quickly realize that there are many viable answers to these complex issues. By questioning each author's conclusions, students and casual readers can begin to develop the critical thinking skills so important to evaluating opinionated material.

Current Controversies is also ideal for controlled research. Each anthology in the series is composed of primary sources taken from a wide gamut of informational categories including periodicals, newspapers, books, US and foreign government documents, and the publications of private and public organizations. Readers will find factual support for reports, debates, and research papers covering all areas of important issues. In addition, an annotated table of contents, an index, a book and periodical bibliography, and a list of organizations to contact are included in each book to expedite further research.

Perhaps more than ever before in history, people are confronted with diverse and contradictory information. During the Persian Gulf War, for example, the public was not only treated to minute-to-minute coverage of the war, it was also inundated with critiques of the coverage and countless analyses of the factors motivating US involvement. Being able to sort through the plethora of opinions accompanying today's major issues, and to draw one's own conclusions, can be a complicated and frustrating struggle. It is the editors' hope that Current Controversies will help readers with this struggle.

# Introduction

"Teenagers have some rights as individuals, but parents have rights also."

The issue of teen privacy surfaces in several areas, including teen relationships with parents, medical care, treatment at school, and with respect to the use of electronic media. Children under the age of eighteen are considered minors in America and, as such, their rights under the law are quite different in many areas than those of adults. The rights of teenagers as they approach adulthood are more controversial than the rights of non-teenage children, however, especially as they relate to privacy. Some of the US Supreme Court decisions on the subject of teen privacy illustrate the controversy about teenagers and their privacy.

The legal right to privacy was first explicitly mentioned by the US Supreme Court in *Griswold v. Connecticut* (1965). The Court in *Griswold* determined that states were not legally allowed to intrude on marital privacy by banning the sale of contraceptives to married people. Although the word "privacy" is never mentioned in the US Constitution, the Court in *Griswold* determined that there was an implicit right to marital privacy that was constitutionally guaranteed. A few years later, the Court extended its understanding of the right to privacy by determining that states could not ban contraceptives for unmarried people. The Court reasoned that there was no good justification for treating married and unmarried persons differently with respect to the right to privacy in matters of reproduction, thus extending the same birth control freedoms identified in *Griswold* to unmarried persons. And in *Carey v. Population Services International* (1977), the Court determined that the right to privacy also applied to minors, preventing states from banning the sale of contraceptives to teenagers sixteen and older. This decision was key in extending the right to privacy under the law to minors.

The legal right to privacy was central to the Court's landmark ruling in *Roe v. Wade* (1973), wherein the Court upheld a woman's right to abortion. In *Planned Parenthood of Central Missouri v. Danforth* (1976), the Court struck down a state law that required parental consent in order for a minor to obtain an abortion, again referencing a minor's right to privacy. This right to privacy, however, is not absolute, and the Court has increasingly allowed state laws that require parental consent for minors to obtain abortions. In *Bellotti v. Baird* (1979), the Court struck down a law requiring minors to obtain informed consent from at least one parent or a court before receiving an abortion. However, the Court noted that a parental consent restriction that allows a judicial bypass—an option for the minor to obtain permission from a court—would be constitutional. In fact, in *Planned Parenthood of Southeastern Pennsylvania v. Casey* (1992), the Court upheld such a law.

Thus, a teenage girl's legal right to privacy with respect to abortion is similar to that of an adult woman, except that states may impose a parental consent requirement. The debate about teenage abortion and parental consent highlights the key point of contention about teen privacy rights: Teenagers have some rights as individuals, but parents have rights also. How these competing rights should be understood in relation to teen privacy is much in dispute.

The right to privacy of teenagers has also been disputed in areas outside of contraception and reproduction, most notably as within public schools. Here, a teenager's right to privacy is in competition with the rights of school officials (acting *in loco parentis*, or in the place of a parent) to maintain order and discipline. In 1985 the US Supreme Court ruled in *New Jersey v. T.L.O.* that although students have some privacy rights at school in their personal belongings, public school officials may search students, if reasonable to maintain discipline at school. Similarly, in *Vernonia School District v. Acton* (1995), the Court again dealt with the issue of student privacy rights. Here, the Court ruled that schools may invade student privacy by requiring drug tests for athletes. The Court extended its ruling in a 2002 decision by allowing schools to drug test students involved in all extracurricular activities.

The above US Supreme Court decisions illustrate some of the controversies surrounding teenagers and privacy that have been debated in the public legal arena. At the core of these debates is the tension between the rights of teenagers to some privacy and the rights of parents (and those acting as parents) to make decisions for minors. The issue continues to be hotly debated in the areas of medical care, student searches, and teen use of new technology. Beyond the legal right of privacy, there is also the moral issue of whether parents should respect teen privacy, a debate that occurs frequently between teenagers and their parents. A wide variety of these hotly debated issues are explored in *Current Controversies: Teens and Privacy*.

# CHAPTER 1

# Do Teens Have a Right to Privacy?

# Chapter Preface

M any teenagers often feel that they do not have enough privacy, especially from their parents. Within the home, minors under the age of eighteen do not have much of a legal right to privacy from their parents. But whether or not they should have some right to privacy that ought to be respected is hotly debated. At the heart of this debate is the issue of how much autonomy teens should have from their parents.

Children naturally have less privacy with their parents than with other individuals. When children are young, they are completely dependent on their parents and the issue of privacy does not arise. As children get older—particularly when they hit the teenage years—they often desire more privacy from their parents. Some may see the denial by parents of teen privacy as an optional child-rearing choice, whereas others may see it as a denial of a right of the teenager. Nonetheless, parents have a great deal of freedom to raise their children as they see fit.

American law has long recognized the fundamental right of parents to direct the upbringing of their child in the manner they desire, within certain guidelines. Parents are responsible for providing the daily necessities of life—food, clothing, and shelter—in addition to education, medical care, and safety. They are free to raise their children in the manner they see fit, short of violating laws that protect children from abuse and neglect. The decision of whether or not to provide children with some degree of privacy at home is, legally at least, up to the parents. In fact, it is the parents' right to privacy that legally has been used to justify their right to raise their children within the above guidelines.

There are various issues that come up between parents and children with respect to privacy. Teenagers may want privacy in the bathroom and their bedrooms. Parents, however, may feel that as long as they are providing the housing for their children, they can enter any room in the house as they deem necessary. Teenagers may not want to tell parents where they are going or who they are talking to on the phone, but parents may feel that it is their right—if not their responsibility—to interfere in order to keep their children safe. Teenagers' use of electronic media such as computers and cell phones is a new point of contention between children and parents. Parents may not want their children using such media when they are not present, and they may feel it is their right to know what websites their children are visiting and who they are texting. Parents and teenagers will likely always debate the extent to which teenagers should have a right to privacy.

# Teens Have a Right to Privacy from Parents

*Melanie Barwick*

*Melanie Barwick is a registered psychologist and health systems scientist in the Community Health Systems Resource Group at the Hospital for Sick Children in Ontario, Canada.*

If you are the parent of a preteen or older, you've stepped into the intersection of adolescence and social media. When I was a teen, I was lucky to have permission to use the phone. Alone time often depended on the number of siblings you had and the space available where you could be on your own. Being a teenager now means you likely have a cell phone, an e-mail account, and a presence on Facebook—at a minimum. Welcome to the land of the digital native—adolescent version.

## Privacy in the Age of Social Media

It's not that our teenagers' need for privacy and autonomy from parents has changed in any way over the decades. Teenagers still pull away, spend more time alone in their rooms, and inflict the mood shifts that come with teen angst. What has changed is that there are now more places for them to enact their privacy needs. This also means that parents need to rethink the privacy boundaries given the new landscape.

Before the World Wide Web, and social media in particular, parents had to contend with an increase in bathroom time, in-the-bedroom-door-closed time, and the mysteries that come with adolescence. Private time existed on the telephone, hanging out in the basement, backyard, park or on the dock—anywhere away from parent view. With the advent of social media, personal space has grown and there are many

Melanie Barwick, "To Peek or Not to Peek: Privacy in the Time of Social Media," *CBC News*, June 29, 2009. Reproduced by permission.

more opportunities for parents to cross the privacy bound-aries—depending on your perspective, of course.

Parenting gurus fall on both sides of the privacy debate. Some espouse a perspective I share, that is to respect kids' privacy. This means, knocking before entering, not going through their bags or knapsacks, not reading their e-mail—indeed, not even knowing their password, and not surreptitiously scanning their text messages when their cell phone is left unattended.

This is not to say I haven't been tempted or slipped up in my resolve to respect their privacy. Know this . . . every breach comes with a price of some sort because you have to deal with anything you learn about your teen's private life without being able to address it with them unless, of course, you're willing to cop to the indiscretion.

---

*I respect my kids' privacy because I think it's the right thing to do.*

---

Mea culpa [my fault]—I have looked in my daughter's school agenda only to find the expected homework notes and slightly shocking graffiti written by her friends. Okay, no big-gie here. Once, driven by my ignorance as a digital immigrant, I sent my daughter a friend request on Facebook: request de-nied! Despite the sting of rejection, it was obvious that this was not the "space" where we would interact and that was okay with me. Of course I worry that her Facebook page might get racier than I would like, but my strategy has been to ask one or two family friends and relatives who have been granted "friend" status to just keep a lookout for anything of concern.

## The Right Thing to Do

In short, I respect my kids' privacy because I think it's the right thing to do, because I would like them to respect my privacy and that of others, and because I believe it promotes a trusting and loving relationship. If it's not okay for your teen to listen in on your phone conversations, read your e-mail, or rifle through your texts or handbag, then it's not okay to behave this way with them. Reading your teen's texts or IMs [instant messages] over their shoulder is the modern-day equivalent of listening in on a phone conversation. The only proviso here is that you can and should act if you suspect they are conversing with a stranger.

Not everyone shares this view. Some experts believe parents should have all access to e-mail passwords and Internet spaces, and that they should let their kids know their activity will be monitored. Some experts make a distinction on the basis of the child's age. For adolescents, studies have shown that children 14 and older think they should have freedom and privacy and parents should respect that, says Mikki Meadows, a professor in Eastern Illinois University's School of Family and Consumer Sciences. For younger children, however, parents should definitely check their e-mail and let the children know they're doing it, she added.

Regardless of where you stand, we all reserve the right to cross that privacy line if and when our teens have gone so far into the adolescent underground that we're no longer in touch with who they are or what they're up to. There may come a point when you may need to infringe on their privacy if you suspect they are at risk. Mitigating risk and harm is one reason why many professionals recommend that kids surf the Web in a family space rather than in their room alone. I occasionally check the Web history on the computer my kids use, just to see where they're surfing—it feels less intrusive than peering over their shoulder and I don't hide the fact that I do it. I've also found nothing of concern, unless you include all the shopping sites that cause me to worry that my income will increasingly end up in the coffers of Hollister and Urban Outfitters!

## Keeping Tabs Without Violating Privacy

Parents should discuss what is and is not appropriate e-mail, text, IM, and Facebook behaviour. As a general rule, let them know that they should not do, say, or post anything in these "spaces" that would be considered inappropriate or risky in a face-to-face context. This includes bullying behaviour. Older teens should be told that many employers conduct Internet searches for online profiles of prospective employees, and will oftentimes make judgments about their trustworthiness and personality based on the content. Be warned: put anything out into cyberspace, including YouTube, and it's there forever.

What kids do in your home is your business, but many would agree that bedrooms and bathrooms are private spaces when in use. The computer they use may be yours, but their space on the Web is theirs. You may be paying for their cell phone and the landline, but their personal communications are private. It is a tricky landscape to master, and we can only hope to approach it as authentically as possible.

Keeping tabs on your teenager needn't be done on the sly. While it's not always easy to stay connected with them at this stage, there are things you can do that will at least sustain the connection you already have. Try to have breakfast or dinner together at least four times a week. While our hectic schedules make this event seem miraculous at times, there is consistent research that supports family meals as important in the development of strong parent-child relationships and family connectedness.

---

*Crossing the privacy boundary may widen the communication chasm between you and your teen.*

---

Like other forms of parental involvement, like playing sports together, family meals are linked to positive teen behaviour. Teens who regularly have meals with their family are less likely to get into fights, think about suicide, smoke, drink, use drugs, and are more likely to have later initiation of sexual activity, and better academic performance than teens who do not. And, more frequent family meals have been found to be associated with less substance use, fewer depressive symptoms, and less suicide involvement, and with better grades.

## Respecting the Privacy Boundary

Crossing the privacy boundary may widen the communication chasm between you and your teen. Here are some suggestions on how to respect your teen's privacy.

- Unless you strongly suspect harmful, illegal, or risky behaviour, don't go through your teen's personal things. Recognizing their personal space will foster a relationship based on trust.

- Getting kids to open up about their personal life is hard, but be delicate. A good place to have sensitive conversations is in the car, alone together. Don't interrogate, regardless of how badly you want to know.

- Give them space, and recognize that public displays of affection are the bane of every teenager. Find other ways to communicate your love, affection, and interest, and do it in private where there is far less risk of embarrassing them.

- Set some rules about bedroom privacy, such as the expectation that you will knock before entering, what they may bring up to their room, and whether you will or will not clean the room—this has implications for what you will do if you find something you do not like in there!

- Consider making the bathroom the only room with a lock on it; locks on bedroom doors are typically not a good idea.

- Let them know you are available if and when they need to talk to you. While it may be difficult to wait for them to come to you with something, if they know you are available, they will be more likely to come to you and share their world.

The caveat to these guidelines is that all teens need to know that while privacy is a right, trust is earned. All parents have a right to know where their teen is when they leave the house so that they can work to ensure their safety.

How you will respect your teen's privacy is something all parents need to think through, and it won't always be easy. The road will be smoother if you work to maintain good communication and a healthy relationship on a regular basis, and the reward will be a mature, respectful teen who uses good coping strategies to navigate their journey into adulthood.

# Children Need Some Places Where They Have Privacy from Adults

*Michael Thompson*

*Michael Thompson is a psychologist specializing in children and families, and he is the author of several books, including* The Pressured Child: Helping Your Child Find Success in School and in Life.

To pry or not to pry? That is the question. As a child psychologist who consults to schools, I am constantly asked questions about what goes on in the minds of children. Parents in particular seem to think that it is always a good thing to know everything about what their kids think and what they do. Recently, I received a phone call from a middle school principal who told me that the parents of his students had become concerned about their children's online activities. They were clueless about what their kids were doing online, and too naive to do anything about it. They told him that they feared the popular social networking website MySpace, and they worried that their kids could be victims of online bullying, or worse. The principal asked if I would visit the school to address these concerns, and I agreed to go.

## The Need for Privacy

Just minutes later, I received an e-mail from the head of an elementary school who took another point of view. "When we were growing up," he wrote, "most of us had a lot of time on our own that we as children filled on our own. I am wondering if one of the reasons that kids spend a great deal of time instant messaging and making websites on MySpace is to cre-

Michael Thompson, "My Turn Online: Leave Kids Alone on the Web," *Newsweek*, September 14, 2006. www.newsweek.com Reproduced by permission.

ate a sense of privacy or a world apart from their parents. We tend to know what the negatives of instant messaging and personal websites might be, but what might the positives be? Maybe we are missing something that we need to keep in mind. Do they need privacy from their parents and, if so, why do they?"

My answer was simple: Yes, children do need privacy. How do you know who you are and what you can do, really do, unless you actually have a chance to be on your own? The most treasured memories of my childhood are walking around the streets of New York City accompanied by my friends, with that precious ticket to freedom—the bus pass—in my pocket.

---

*We cannot bear the anxiety of not knowing everything about our children's whereabouts in the physical world.*

---

Other sweet memories were from July and August, when I spent hours away from my parents near a lake in southern Massachusetts accompanied by friends and cousins. We played for hours; we built forts and fought imaginary enemies. Did we do some bad things? Sure, I guess so. My friends and I blew up some bullfrogs with firecrackers. We tried smoking cigarettes; we made some illicit campfires. We even talked some girls into playing "doctor." All of this before I was 11 years old.

## The Lack of Private Time

Would my parents have been upset if they had known what we were doing? Without a doubt. Did we take some risks? Certainly. I don't know whether I'd be better or worse off had I taken less risks as a child, but I do know that I cannot imagine my childhood without those times. I cannot conceive of my adult personality without those memories.

Kids today spend almost no time "in the woods," and their moments spent away from their parents' watchful gaze are precious and few. In our middle- and upper-middle-class neighborhoods, children are largely indoors, taking lessons doing homework and getting ready to go to town sports. They are endlessly supervised and monitored. How many parents today are willing to do what our parents did: shovel us out the door at noon, saying "Don't come back until 6 o'clock?"

We cannot bear the anxiety of not knowing everything about our children's whereabouts in the physical world. So our children wander off into cyberspace, killing zombies, talking to strangers and visiting all kinds of websites, weird and stupid and sexy. And they know we don't have the time, attention or expertise to follow them there. The Internet is often the only private place for a child today.

## A Careful Balance

That isn't to say that parents and administrators should turn a blind eye to their children's online activities, they shouldn't. To the middle school principal, I suggested he ask his computer teacher to go online and check out the MySpace pages of all of his students. After all, a middle school director in Maryland I worked with found that two of his girls had posted photos of themselves in their underwear, and their parents knew nothing about it. We need to be vigilant.

But I'm always torn when people call me for wise counsel about kids and privacy, because roaming around in my head there is still a child who treasures his private adventures. My inner boy is certainly going to shout, "Let them be! Let them take some risks." The parent in me is going to worry and advise, "Check their websites. There are dangers out there. There are pedophiles on the Internet." And what about the psychologist in me?

I hope my inner psychologist has the courage to remember his own boyhood and to keep reminding parents of how precious a bit of privacy was to them when they were growing up.

# Teens Should Have a Right to Privacy That Is Earned

*Kelly Weber*

*Kelly Weber was a senior at Westwood Regional High School and editor for the* Cardinal Chronicle, *the school newspaper, when this piece was written.*

Privacy is a very important part of anyone's life. Everyone has the right to keep a few things to themselves. Teenagers, especially, have the right to privacy, and I believe that sometimes we do not get enough.

## The Benefits of Privacy

Throughout my high school career, I have earned my parents' trust. They know that I will do the right thing without too much interference or intervention from them. I was never forced to show them my homework or every graded assignment I got back; instead, I shared with them only what I chose to.

They would inquire about my day at school, but I was never hassled for every single detail. Of course, if I had a problem, they would help me with whatever I needed, but if I said everything was going fine, they believed me.

I think that fact helped me accomplish everything that I have. By giving me privacy as far as my schoolwork was concerned, they allowed me to make my own mistakes and achieve everything truly on my own. They were never on top of me to do my homework or study for a big test; it was simply expected that I would. I was encouraged and motivated by the fact that my parents chose to treat me like an adult, and worked hard to live up to their expectations.

Kelly Weber, "Teens Who Expect Privacy at Home, School Must Earn It," *Record* (Bergen County, NJ), January 26, 2010, p. L2. Reproduced by permission.

## Privacy Is Earned

It is important to note that I was given this privacy because I earned it. I had never given my parents a reason to not trust that I would do my very best in school. If I had given them an indication that my progress needed to be monitored, they would have watched me like a hawk. However, since I always did well in school, they rarely questioned me about my studies.

---

*A little trust goes a long way.*

---

The same idea applies at school. In all the years that I have been attending school, I have never once felt that my privacy was violated. In fact, the only time anyone's privacy is violated, like having their locker searched, is when they have aroused some sort of suspicion. Like at home, if you earn your privacy at school, you will receive it.

I believe that teenagers need privacy in order to succeed. Being treated like a child is an excuse for a teenager to act like one. If someone is constantly supervised, there is no motivation for them to take personal responsibility or to do anything on their own. I've found that when teenagers are treated like adults, they will rise to the occasion and act like one.

## Teenagers and Parents

So, fellow teenagers, make sure that you earn the privacy that you crave. You can do this really easily: Just do what you say you're going to do. Try hard in school. Study for a big test days in advance, without being asked. Do your homework at your actual home, and put effort into it. Your relationship with your parents and your grades will both be better for it.

Parents, go ahead and give your children a little space. When you ask about their day and they give you a one-word response, let it go. If you know your child is a responsible student and an all-around good kid, believe that they are doing the right thing. A little trust goes a long way. If your child knows that you trust and believe in them, I guarantee that they will work twice as hard to validate your decision.

# Teens Do Not Have a Right to Privacy from Parents

*Lindsay Ferrier*

*Lindsay Ferrier is the author of the parenting blog* Suburban Turmoil.

Parenting teenagers has honed my detective skills to the sharpness of a No. 2 pencil on the first day of school. When my girls mention a new kid in their social circle, I do my best to act casual. But the moment I get a spare second, I'm on the Internet, pulling up his online profile, perusing his contacts and scouring tagged photos of him for any evidence of impropriety. "His Friends list leaves much to be desired," I told Hubs one night not long ago, after he mentioned a new addition to my stepdaughters' group of friends. "Corey Green. Mark Hamilton. Jay Stallings. Stoners, all of them. And look, here's a picture of him laying on a sofa with Rebecca *Stevens*?! She's, like, a total slut!" I look up at Hubs, exasperated. "This is *not* someone we want the girls hanging out with." "How do you know all this?" Hubs asks.

## A Spying Parent

"Facebook, Hubs," I say dismissively. "Welcome to the new millennium."

When we score an address, which is information we require when the girls are going to someone's home, I can go a step further. Armed only with a street name and number, I can get property tax records, which tell me the kids' parents' names and how much they paid for the house. A Google Maps search provides me with a street-level photo of exactly where the girls are headed. Not long ago, that happened to be a

Lindsay Ferrier, "Respect Your Teens' Privacy? Not on Their Lives," *Nashville Scene*, November 19, 2009. www.nashvillescene.com. Reproduced by permission.

home belonging to a local music mogul. I did a search for his name and found an online publication featuring pictures of the home's interior at another party on the premises, this one for celebrity guests instead of inebriated teenagers.

---

*I view the relationship between a parent and a teen's privacy as similar to that of an employer and employee.*

---

"I hope they enter through the foyer," I murmured to Hubs, enlarging the photos. "There's a Kandinsky [a painting by Russian artist Wassily Kandinsky] in there I would *love* for them to see." I consider texting them, DID U SEE KANDIN-SKY IN ENTRANCE? But in the end, I decided against it. I didn't want to blow my Clueless Parent façade.

It's a complicated situation, though, because they're my *step*daughters. I may love them as I do my own children, but that doesn't mean I have the same rights and privileges as my husband when it comes to rearing them, and Hubs thinks they deserve their privacy. So with them, I mostly limit my spying to what's publicly available on the Net.

## The Parental Relationship

As far as my own kids are concerned, though, when it comes to their privacy, the moment I suspect something's amiss, all bets are off.

I view the relationship between a parent and a teen's privacy as similar to that of an employer and employee. In the workplace, we operate under the impression that our employers may at any time secretly monitor our phone conversations, our e-mails, our computer usage and our on-the-job behavior. Most employers don't do this on a daily basis, but we know the possibility is there if suspicions are raised. I plan to tell my kids to conduct themselves in the exact same way. I'm not interested in monitoring their actions 24-7 when they're older—I'm getting my fill of that with them right now. But they should know that at any time, I may be watching or listening if I suspect they're up to no good.

## A Divergence of Views

I realize there are plenty of parents (and even more teenagers) out there who'd disagree with me. Teen privacy is a touchy subject, and whenever I hear opinions on the issue, they run the gamut. In a recent online message board discussion I read on teens' privacy, parents were divided, 50-50.

"One thing that I have always made a conscious effort of in raising my son (who is now 16) is to respect his privacy," wrote one mom. "I will never enter his room without knocking, I don't go through his things if I'm 'looking' for something. I ask him for what I need if it is in his room. If he's not home, I wait."

Another mom countered: "I feel parents this day and age need all the inside information possible to help teens stay safe and healthy. Many times I hear from parents in shock when their child's mental health has deteriorated, they are cutting themselves or taking drugs or are depressed. We never saw it coming, they say. Would a peek into a diary have foretold and they could have done something about it?"

Most interesting to me was a statement from Katie Allison Granju, a parenting author from Knoxville [Tennessee], whose eldest daughter is now 18. In a recent appearance on ABC-News.com, Katie said that looking back on raising her firstborn, "I had a misplaced sense of a teenager's right to privacy, I think. I was a little uncomfortable with violating privacy. I'm not really uncomfortable with that at all anymore. If I have any suspicion that one of my children is in trouble, I'm going to be looking into everything, and they know that."

Been there, been converted. And that's enough for me to keep my Sherlock Holmes hat handy for years to come.

# To Be a Good Parent, It Is Necessary to Invade Teen Privacy

**Chronicle**

*The* Chronicle *is a daily newspaper in Toowoomba, Australia.*

Who had died and made him boss?

No one, that's who. I am allowed—because I am your father.

And that's precisely what he told his daughter when she declared—with many tears and much melodramatic hand-wringing—that he had ruined her social life and destroyed her precious teenage rights.

Personally, I applauded him.

## The Exercise of Parental Rights

Watching as he approached the schoolboy who has sent an offensive text message to his daughter, I could hardly refrain from cheering out loud when he said "if you ever use language like that around my girl again, I'll be talking to your parents. And then the principal. Then the police".

The ultra-cool facade of the young man hardly slipped, but he must have been abashed. Sure, the iPod didn't come out of his ears, but his fingers did slip mid-text.

The daughter, trying her best to sink below the level of the dashboard as she took in the scene, was mortified.

"You have invaded my privacy! You have embarrassed me in front of my friends! I hate you! I never asked to be born!"

Yawn. As a spectator, the drama queen antics bored me.

*Chronicle* (Toowoomba, Australia), "Invading the Private World of Teens Can Be Necessary," October 29, 2009, p. 21. Reproduced by permission.

But how entertaining it was to watch a father exercise his parental rights, take control, and act in his little girl's best interests despite the ugly response he knew would ensue. I could clearly see discipline envy writ large on the faces of other mums [mothers] near me.

---

*I think kids have way too much privacy these days.*

---

It is so rare, you see. So caught up are we in acknowledging the rights of our teenage children that we often forget our own rights as parents to do whatever it takes to keep those same kids safe from the world—even if the threat is as supposedly innocuous as a cheeky pimply boy who didn't stop to think he might get busted.

## An Overfocus on Privacy

I realised the truth of this statement at a recent gathering of friends, when I casually said that I regularly visit my children's Facebook sites and would have no moral issue with reviewing their mobile phone messages, e-mail in-boxes or Internet histories should I ever feel the need.

I pay the bills, I said, and it is my job to ensure they are not being exposed to people or situations they do not possess the maturity or decision-making skills to handle.

The subsequent silence was palpable.

"But what about their right to privacy?" someone eventually squeaked to nods around the table.

Well, call me a helicopter mum, call me obsessive, call me overbearing (none of the titles are new; I have two teenage children) but I think kids have way too much privacy these days.

When I was growing up, my parents knew exactly who was calling me. Phones weren't cordless; we had to conduct our conversations in full hearing of the family. When we watched television, we did it all together in one room. We had no e-mail, Internet or MSN [Microsoft Network]. We went to our rooms only to read a book, throw a tantrum, or sleep.

These days, kids can have conversations with faceless, nameless friends during dinner, on the way to school, in bed, on the loo [toilet]—and you don't even know it's going on. They possess instant access to the world and form relationships without even meeting. They hide in their rooms with their private televisions, private computers, private phone lines. They live in enormous houses where you can go for hours without crossing paths with another person. They inhabit secretive worlds from which it is easy to keep parents out with an angst-filled scowl and liberal use of the word "private".

## The Need for Parental Responsibility

Yes, teenagers need space to grow as individuals, to express opinions without running the risk of parental disapproval, to develop relationships in their own way, to be themselves.

But the price of this liberty need not be the abandonment of all parental responsibility.

We moan when we hear of cyberbullying, and quake in our boots at the notion of online predators. We wonder what our children were looking at as they quickly minimise the screen when we walk in the room, and we worry that a missed keystroke could transport them to a world we wish didn't exist.

Despite this, we maintain that we have no right to take control. We fear the backlash from our kids, we fear being parentally incorrect.

All of which is bollocks [nonsense].

We can't have it both ways. Either we take a tougher line and protect our kids to some extent, or we give them all the privacy and personal space they so righteously declare is their entitlement and then suffer the consequences.

I'm with the chap down at the local school. By enraging his daughter he is defending her. As parents, we all need to create a little more teenage rage.

# CHAPTER 2

# Should Teens Have Privacy in Receiving Medical Care?

# Overview: Minors and Privacy in Medical Care

## Guttmacher Institute

*The Guttmacher Institute is a nonprofit organization focused on sexual and reproductive health research, policy analysis, and public education.*

The legal ability of minors to consent to a range of sensitive health care services—including sexual and reproductive health care, mental health services and alcohol and drug abuse treatment—has expanded dramatically over the past 30 years. This trend reflects the recognition that, while parental involvement in minors' health care decisions is desirable, many minors will not avail themselves of important services if they are forced to involve their parents. With regard to sexual and reproductive health care, many states explicitly permit all or some minors to obtain contraceptive, prenatal and STI [sexually transmitted infections] services without parental involvement. Moreover, nearly every state permits minor parents to make important decisions on their own regarding their children. In sharp contrast, the majority of states require parental involvement in a minor's abortion.

In most cases, state consent laws apply to all minors age 12 and older. In some cases, however, states allow only certain groups of minors—such as those who are married, pregnant or already parents—to consent. Several states have no relevant policy or case law; in these states, physicians commonly provide medical care without parental consent to minors they deem mature, particularly if the state allows minors to consent to related services. . . .

Guttmacher Institute, "An Overview of Minors' Consent Law," *State Policies in Brief*, April 1, 2010. Reproduced by permission.

# Minors' Consent Law

- *Contraceptive Services*: 26 states and the District of Columbia allow all minors (12 and older) to consent to contraceptive services. 21 states allow only certain categories of minors to consent to contraceptive services. 4 states have no relevant policy or case law.

- *STI Services*: All states and the District of Columbia allow all minors to consent to STI services. 18 of these states allow, but do not require, a physician to inform a minor's parents that he or she is seeking or receiving STI services when the doctor deems it in the minor's best interests.

- *Prenatal Care*: 32 states and the District of Columbia explicitly allow all minors to consent to prenatal care. Another state allows a minor to consent to prenatal care during the 1st trimester; requires parental consent for most care during the 2nd and 3rd trimesters. 13 of these states allow, but do not require, a physician to inform parents that their minor daughter is seeking or receiving prenatal care when the doctor deems it in the minor's best interests. 4 additional states allow a minor who can be considered "mature" to consent. 13 states have no relevant policy or case law.

- *Adoption*: 28 states and the District of Columbia allow all minor parents to choose to place their child for adoption. In addition, 5 states require the involvement of a parent and 5 states require the involvement of legal counsel. The remaining 12 states have no relevant policy or case law.

- *Medical Care for a Child*: 30 states and the District of Columbia allow all minor parents to consent to medical care for their child. The remaining 20 states have no relevant explicit policy or case law.

- *Abortion*: 3 states and the District of Columbia explicitly allow all minors to consent to abortion services. 22 states require that at least one parent consent to a minor's abortion, while 11 states require prior notification of at least one parent. 4 states require both notification of and consent from a parent prior to a minor's abortion. 7 additional states have parental involvement laws that are temporarily or permanently enjoined. 6 states have no relevant policy or case law.

# Confidential Health Care for Teens Is Good Policy

*Scott J. Spear and Abigail English*

*Scott J. Spear is medical director of Planned Parenthood of Central Texas. Abigail English is director of the Center for Adolescent Health & the Law in Chapel Hill, North Carolina.*

Parents want their adolescent children to be healthy and safe; and society wants healthy adolescents who will grow into healthy adults. These statements may be truisms, but they are essential to recognize in the ongoing debates about confidential health services for adolescents. In spite of broad consistency among health care professional guidelines, research findings and legal protections, the debates continue. Too often the dialogue deteriorates into a harangue, even though there is much room for agreement among the vast majority of parents, policy makers and health care professionals. Advocates on both sides—proponents of confidential care for adolescents and supporters of mandated parental involvement—both claim the high ground but rarely find common ground. This must change. For that to happen, more attention needs to focus on the ways in which the interests of adolescents, parents, health care providers and society coincide rather than conflict.

## The Debate About Adolescent Confidentiality

Current efforts to limit confidentiality protections for adolescent health care, and particularly for sexual and reproductive health services, originated with laws first enacted three decades ago. Since that time, most states—with California and a

Scott J. Spear and Abigail English, "Protecting Confidentiality to Safeguard Adolescents' Health: Finding Common Ground," *Contraception*, vol. 76, no. 2, August 2007, pp. 73–76. Reproduced by permission.

handful of others being notable exceptions—have been successful in restricting access to abortion by minors without parental consent, parental notification or involvement by a court. Although the issue of confidential access to abortion for adolescents has been the most visible and the most frequently litigated, ongoing efforts to limit access to other confidential sexual and reproductive health care—for birth control and even STD [sexually transmitted disease] services—have been deliberated and determined in Congress and numerous state legislatures. When these efforts have not succeeded, the reason has often been that parents who want their adolescents to be healthy and safe are helped to understand that restricting confidential care will put adolescents' health and safety at risk rather than furthering them. This approach was recently effective in California in defeating a ballot proposition that would have amended the state constitution to require parental notification for minors' abortions.

---

*Beginning to make important health care decisions is helpful to adolescents for many reasons.*

---

There is no doubt that the notion of requiring parental consent or notification for adolescents' health care—especially when that care is related to sexual or reproductive health—seems initially appealing to many parents and policy makers. Even the most sanguine parents may feel that requiring their consent for health care for their adolescent is beneficent given the frequent recitation of frightening statistics about STDs and teen pregnancy and youth violence—even though the "epidemic" aspects of these problems are often overstated by the media. There are other reasons that mandates for parental involvement may seem appealing: Some parents worry about losing control as their children move into adolescence; while others believe it is their right to be involved. Ultimately, however, many parents come to understand the importance of confidential care when they learn that it will not only help to protect their children's health but also help them learn to make responsible decisions as they move towards adulthood.

Providing confidential care to adolescents is consistent with what we know about adolescent development, what we can learn from research about the effect of limiting confidentiality, what is embodied in health care professionals' ethical guidelines and policies, and what the law requires.

## Healthy Adolescent Development

Those of us in the health field who care for adolescents have a responsibility to share what we know about adolescent development with parents who are trying to raise healthy young people. Beginning to make important health care decisions is helpful to adolescents for many reasons. Most 15-, 16- and 17-year-olds—and in some cases younger teens—are cognitively and emotionally mature enough to understand the consequences of their actions regarding health concerns and are capable of giving informed consent to health care. Permitting and encouraging them to do so with trusted health care professionals helps them develop the skills needed to become healthy adults.

Some parents, and some adolescents, have difficulty letting go of close parental involvement in health care decisions even after adolescents have become adults. Many health care professionals caring for college students are familiar with the phenomenon of "helicopter parents" hovering over children who are legally adults, but who often abdicate important decisions to their parents rather than take responsibility themselves. Assisting young people during adolescence to begin developing the capacity to make their own decisions about health care, with guidance from trusted professionals and other adults, can serve them well as they enter adulthood and need to act responsibly and independently with respect to their own health care.

Failing to help young people acquire these skills can impede their developing the ability to make sound health care decisions and retard their essential maturation process of becoming a healthy adult. As health care professionals, we can and should help caring parents foster healthy development in their teenagers by aiding them in understanding that to raise responsible future citizens who can function in a complex society without constant parental assistance, they must give adolescents increasing responsibility at the appropriate developmental stages.

## The Privacy Concerns of Adolescents

A body of research conducted over the past few decades has consistently found that privacy is a significant concern for adolescents and that privacy concerns influence many aspects of their interactions with the health care system. Concerns about whether care will be confidential—and specifically whether their parents will be informed—can determine whether adolescents forgo care entirely, which providers and sites they visit, whether they are candid in disclosing their health history and which services they will accept.

The full picture as portrayed by the evidence from research is complex and nuanced, particularly with respect to sexual and reproductive health services. On the one hand, several studies have documented that a majority of adolescents using family planning clinics do so with their parents' knowledge, or even at their explicit suggestion. On the other hand, many adolescents say they would not use the clinic or would avoid certain services if their parents had to be notified. Moreover, the vast majority of adolescents will not modify their health behaviors as a result of mandated parental notification—only 1% would stop having sex if parental notification were mandated for contraception, for example, and two in 10 would forgo contraception entirely or would rely on the withdrawal method. Of minors whose parents did not know they were at the clinic, 70% said they would not use the clinic for prescription contraception if parental notification were required.

---

*The importance of confidentiality in adolescent health care has long been recognized by health care professionals.*

---

The impact on health outcomes of decreases in confidentiality protection has not been extensively studied, but the available evidence suggests that adverse effects are likely. For example, a study of Texas policies to require parental consent for state-funded family planning services and to increase reporting of adolescents' sexual activity estimated that public costs for increases in teen pregnancies and STDs could be as high as $44 million annually. An Illinois study examined the effects of one county's implementation of a parental-consent requirement for contraception and found an increase in the proportion of births to females under age 19 in that county, despite a decrease during the same period in nearby counties that had similar racial and economic profiles and no restrictions on minors' access to contraception. . . .

## The Importance of Confidentiality

The impact of mandated parental involvement appears to be significant and potentially risky for adolescents' health. Nevertheless, most adolescents seek health care—including sexual and reproductive health services—with their parents' knowledge. So, it is essential for parents, policy makers and health care professionals to understand that not all adolescents require confidential care at all times; indeed, many share information with their parents. But for those who do need confidentiality protections at some point in their adolescence, or for specific services, those protections need to be in place.

The importance of confidentiality in adolescent health care has long been recognized by health care professionals. Virtually every organization of health care professionals has incorporated into its policies and codes of ethics statements about the need to protect confidentiality in health care generally, the important role it plays in adolescent care and the kinds of protections that are needed for specific services and for special populations of adolescents. The consistency among these statements is remarkable and reflects both an appreciation of the research findings and an awareness of the legal framework.

## Legal Support for Confidentiality

An extensive body of laws has been developed over the past half century that supports adolescents' access to confidential health care based on their own consent. The existing legal framework includes constitutional protections at the federal and state level, requirements of federal funding programs, privacy regulations issued under the federal Health Insurance Portability and Accountability Act that are often referred to as the HIPAA Privacy Rule, and elements of minor consent and medical privacy laws delineated by the states.

In a series of decisions dating back more than 30 years, the constitutional right of privacy has been held to protect minors as well as adults. Specifically, the right of privacy protects minors' decisions whether to "bear or beget" a child and extends to both contraception and abortion. Although minors' right of privacy is not absolute and the state has greater authority to control the conduct of children and restrict their privacy than it can for adults, the protections currently in place are significant. Supreme Court rulings have determined that a state may not require parental consent or notification for abortion without providing an alternative such as a judicial bypass that allows mature minors to make their own decisions without involving their parents. A state is also limited in the extent to which it can constitutionally restrict minors' access to contraceptives. Similar, and in some instances greater, protections for adolescents' privacy rights have also been found in state constitutions.

Two federal programs that provide funding for family planning services have long protected confidential access for adolescents. Since 1970, the federal Title X Family Planning program has provided confidential family planning services to low-income women and adolescents. The Title X regulations contain strong confidentiality protections and these extend to adolescents as well as adults. Efforts by states to require parental consent for Title X–funded services have been struck down by the courts. Sexually active adolescents who are eligible for Medicaid also have a right to receive family planning services on a confidential basis. Federal Medicaid law precludes states from requiring parental consent for minors to access family planning services.

## Common Interests in Confidentiality

The federal HIPAA Privacy Rule also protects minors as well as adults. Minors who are legally able to consent for their own health care are generally treated by the rule as individuals who are protected in their own right. However, on the issue of parents' access to their children's protected health information, the HIPAA Privacy Rule defers to "state or other applicable law." Thus, to the extent that minors' confidentiality is protected by specific state or federal laws—such as the myriad state minor consent laws that exist in every state, the medical privacy laws in some states, or Title X and Medicaid—it is protected by HIPAA also. However, to the extent that, for example, state laws are silent or explicitly allow health care professionals to disclose information to parents, the HIPAA Privacy Rule allows that to occur. In such circumstances, the discretion of the health care professionals should be guided not only by the legal framework, but also by the policies and ethical guidelines of health care professional organizations, the findings from research and their knowledge of adolescent development. Doing so will enable them to strike an appropriate balance between protecting adolescents' interest in confidentiality and involving parents when that is necessary to protect adolescents' health. Indeed, the commentary in the preamble to the HIPAA Privacy Rule explicitly states that it "does not want to interfere with the professional requirements ... or other ethical codes of health care providers with respect to the confidentiality of health information or with the health care practices of such providers with respect to adolescent health care."

Looking back over the past half century and reviewing the research findings about the effect of limiting confidentiality on health-seeking behaviors and health outcomes for adolescents, together with the policies and ethical guidelines of health care professionals and the long-standing legal framework for confidentiality, we can see that there is a remarkable consensus about the important role of confidentiality protections in safeguarding the health of adolescents. Dedicated health care professionals who care for adolescents, concerned parents who are trying to raise adolescents to become healthy and safe adults, policy makers who are trying to further society's interest in the development of productive and responsible citizens, and adolescents themselves all essentially have common interests that can provide the basis for finding common ground in the ongoing public discussions about confidentiality in adolescent health care.

# Teens Should Be Allowed an Abortion Without Parental Consent

*Kate Michelman*

*Kate Michelman is the former president of NARAL Pro-Choice America and author of* With Liberty and Justice for All: A Life Spent Protecting the Right to Choose.

It had all the hallmarks of a pre-*Roe v. Wade* tragedy: a desperate young woman, an illegal abortion, a promising life truncated by a shortsighted law that assumed politicians, rather than women, knew best. But when Becky Bell, a high school junior, died of an illegal abortion, the year was neither 1958 nor 1968. It was 1988, fifteen years after *Roe* declared that the constitutional right to privacy guaranteed a woman's right to choose abortion safely and legally.

## The Danger of State-Mandated Parental Consent

Becky lived in Indiana, where state law required that young women seeking abortions obtain permission from either their parents or a judge. The family was close, but—like many teenagers—Becky was afraid of disappointing them by revealing the pregnancy. The idea of appearing before a judge, discussing this intimate situation with a complete stranger who was in a position of authority, must have been terrifying as well. Rather than go to court, Becky had an illegal abortion. A few days later, she complained of feeling sick. At first, her parents thought she had pneumonia or the flu. Her fever spiked to 104. By the time her parents got her to the emergency room, Becky was so weak they had to carry her inside.

Kate Michelman, *With Liberty and Justice for All: A Life Spent Protecting the Right to Choose*. Penguin, 2005, pp. 83–87. Reproduced by permission.

Her mother later recounted what happened when they arrived: "I heard the nurses say her veins had collapsed. They put oxygen on her, but Becky pulled the mask off. I leaned down and said, 'Honey, tell Mom, tell me, honey.' She said, 'Mom, Dad, I love you, forgive me.' And that was it. Her heart stopped."

I met Becky's parents, Bill and Karen Bell, in late 1989. We were each testifying before a committee of the Michigan House of Representatives that was considering a parental consent law. Michigan's governor at the time, Jim Blanchard, was strongly pro-choice, but Michigan's antichoice movement was one of the most aggressive and well organized in the country. The antichoice movement was pressuring the legislature to pass a measure they believed would seem reasonable. Who, after all, does not agree that parents should be involved in their daughters' decisions? But the Bells knew the issue was more complicated. They had agreed to travel throughout the country to tell their story so legislators and others would understand the real dangers of state-mandated parental consent and notification laws. Their willingness to speak out is one of the most personally courageous, selfless acts I have ever seen.

## One Family's Position

I already knew the Bells' story, but I was nonetheless heartbroken meeting them for the first time. As a mother, I could only imagine the pain they must have endured. Before the Michigan hearing began, I saw Bill and Karen across the room. Bill is a big, blond, garrulous man, the kind whose warmth envelopes you. Karen is more reserved than Bill, but every bit as engaging and caring. Bill was interested in politics, but neither of them was politically active before Becky's death, and certainly not on this issue. They were friendly, middle class, and hardworking. If a tragedy like Becky's death could happen to them, it could happen to anyone. I walked up, introduced myself, and embraced them both.

"I'm just devastated for you," I said. "As a mother, I don't know how you bear the pain. It must be very hard to tell Becky's story, but I want you to know how grateful we are that you're willing to talk about your experience so that it doesn't happen again to another family. I don't know how to thank you for what you're doing."

---

*Parental involvement laws would certainly sound reasonable to me, as a mother, if I did not know the harm such requirements can cause.*

---

Bill was in tears as he evoked painful memories. "At first, we were not sure about telling our story. But we needed to give some meaning to this tragedy. Nothing can make up for this loss, but we have to try to salvage some good from it by making sure society learns from Becky's death."

## Parental Involvement Laws

State-mandated parental involvement laws like the one Michigan was considering are emblematic of a tactic the antichoice movement has employed since *Roe v. Wade* was decided. Rather than trying to ban abortion outright, which most politicians acknowledge the American public does not support, they instead chip away at the right to choose, one restriction at a time. In the case of parental involvement laws, antichoice legislators—for all their claims about promoting family values—are not social workers or family therapists. They are politicians intent on bending the law to their own purposes and denying women the right to choose regardless of the consequences. They take complicated issues and reduce them to emotional, highly charged rhetoric and simplistic solutions that often sound perfectly reasonable on the surface.

Parental involvement laws would certainly sound reasonable to me as a mother, if I did not know the harm such requirements can cause. Having raised three daughters, I also

53

know how challenging parenting teens can be, especially when it involves issues of their emerging sexuality. Antichoice politicians believe government can and should force families to communicate regardless of the fact that family communication is sometimes nonexistent or dysfunctional. Even in families where communication is healthy, teenagers become more private at exactly the same time they become aware of their sexual feelings.

My daughters certainly did. I thought we had as close and open a relationship as parents and children can have, but throughout adolescence our communications were often strained. It worried me, as it does many parents. I worked hard to keep the lines of communication open. I talked frankly with them about responsible sexual behavior and especially their right to say no to sex.

---

*Government cannot mandate healthy family communication, and politicians should not risk the health and lives of teens by interfering in private family matters.*

---

## The Issue of Teen Communication

But I was the one doing the talking, not the girls, and that's the key. The simple fact is that a high percentage of teens say they are sexually active, and not all of them talk to their parents. All parents assume their own daughter would tell them about a pregnancy, and the reality is that a majority voluntarily do so. The younger the teen, the likelier she is to involve her parents in a decision about pregnancy. Many young women who do not involve a parent have good reasons, including the fear of abuse or being kicked out of their homes. Pregnancies that are the result of rape or incest add an especially tragic dimension to the problem.

The idea that young women who are unable to talk with their parents should be forced to appear like criminals before a judge is absurd. Many adolescent women are confronted with abusive judges. A Louisiana judge asked one such young woman what she would say to her fetus if she had the abortion. Another judge in Ohio refused to grant permission for an abortion to a seventeen-year-old college-bound student because she "had not had enough hard knocks in her life." Their condescension is outdone only by the irony: Girls willing to endure judicial hearings to obtain an abortion because they believe they are not ready for motherhood are actually engaging in one of the most mature and thoughtful acts of their lives.

Ideally, of course, teenagers *will* talk with their parents about being pregnant. But government cannot mandate healthy family communication, and politicians should not risk the health and lives of teens by interfering in private family matters. The real question is what society can do to educate young people about sexuality, and thereby reduce the number of adolescent pregnancies and the need for abortion. And in cases where young women do not talk to their parents and are unwilling to see a judge, should we risk their lives by denying medically safe abortions? These are complex issues that do not have easy solutions.

I understand the swirl of emotions parents feel, and I respect the fact that there are divergent views on this question. Many people have counseled me to drop the issue. It's futile, they insist, and it makes the pro-choice movement look extreme. After all, who could possibly be against a law mandating that parents be involved in something as serious as choosing an abortion? My answer is: anyone who knows Bill and Karen Bell.

# Contraceptives Should Be Available to Teens Without Parental Consent

*Center for Reproductive Rights*

*The Center for Reproductive Rights is an organization that uses the law to advance reproductive freedom as a fundamental human right.*

Currently, no state or federal laws require minors to get parental consent in order to get contraception. Increasingly, however, proposals are being introduced to restrict teens' access to reproductive health care by calling for parental consent or notification.

## Parental Consent or Notification Proposals

Teens in a variety of circumstances would be affected if required to obtain parental consent for contraception:

- A young woman seeking contraception from a clinic—birth control pills, Depo-Provera, diaphragm—would be forced to obtain parental permission.

- A minor who buys condoms at a pharmacy could be turned away without parental consent.

- A teen who seeks emergency contraception because of forced or unanticipated intercourse would need approval, even though emergency contraception must be used within 72 hours of unprotected intercourse.

Center for Reproductive Rights, "Parental Consent and Notice for Contraceptives Threatens Teen Health and Constitutional Rights," November 1, 2006. www.reproductiverights.org. Reproduced by permission.

Two types of mandatory parental contact for contraception are sometimes proposed:

- Mandatory parental consent would force teenagers to get permission from one or two parents before getting contraception.

- Mandatory parental notification would require young people to tell one or two parents about their plans to get contraception. Mandatory notification poses the same danger of discouraging contraceptive use by teens, as does the requirement of consent. If a minor is fearful about discussing contraception with a parent, there is no difference between "telling" the parent and getting parental permission.

## Federal Programs Require Confidentiality for Teens

Two federal programs—Title X [Family Planning program] and Medicaid—protect teens' privacy and prohibit parental consent requirements for teens seeking contraception. Title X provides funds to states for family planning services; Medicaid covers health care services for low-income women. Both programs mandate that, in exchange for receiving monies from the federal government, health care services treat all patients confidentially, including teens.

Attempts by states to implement parental consent requirements for contraceptive services that are funded by these programs have been invalidated when challenged in court. Courts find that the requirements impermissibly conflict with federal program requirements. Federal program rules mandating confidentiality preempt state efforts to make new requirements. Nevertheless, states have continued to introduce legislation that would mandate parental involvement in teens' private contraceptive decisions.

Parental contact requirements discourage teens from seeking contraception, even though they may already be sexually active. Confidentiality can be a determining factor for teens deciding whether or not to seek contraceptive protection.

## Teenagers Need Access to Contraceptive Services

Almost half of women in the United States have intercourse by the time they turn 18. While the teen pregnancy rate today has dropped slightly in the past twenty years, almost one million teens become pregnant each year. A sexually active teen using no contraception has a 90% chance of becoming pregnant within a one-year period, according to the Guttmacher Institute.

Lack of contraception increases the chances of unintended pregnancy. Nearly 80% of teen pregnancies are unplanned in the U.S. Teen pregnancy rates are much higher in the U.S. than in other industrial countries—double the rates in England; nine times as high as the Netherlands. Lack of contraception also increases the possibility of exposure to sexually transmitted diseases. About three million U.S. teens acquire a sexually transmitted infection every year.

Supporters of measures forcing teens to notify or get consent from their parents argue that they promote the best interests of young women and improve family communications.

These arguments are out of touch with reality. These proposed laws threaten adolescent health and well-being. Even teens who could comply with parental consent requirements will face delays in getting contraceptive services. Additional clinic visits, missed school or work time, and increased expense will result.

Many young women live in nontraditional situations— with one parent, a stepparent, other relatives, or on their own. Contact with biological parents, if required by law, may be impossible.

Some teens face violence or other severe consequences from parents as a result of informing their parents that they are seeking contraceptive services. Minors fearful of retribution may forgo using contraception altogether, even though they are already sexually active.

Teens who seek contraceptive services are generally sexually active already. They benefit from meeting with health care providers who can provide screening, counseling about sexually transmitted diseases, and education about other reproductive health concerns.

---

*Minors have a right to privacy that includes their ability to use contraception.*

---

## Minors' Right to Privacy

Several courts have found that state parental consent requirements may not be imposed on federally funded family planning programs. Where states accept Title X and Medicaid funds, they cannot require minors to obtain parental consent prior to using those services.

Minors have a right to privacy that includes their ability to use contraception.

The U.S. Supreme Court said in 1977 that denial of contraception is not a permissible way to deter sexual activity.

Courts that have addressed attempts to impose parental consent or notification requirements have found that these types of laws conflict with a minor's constitutional right to privacy.

Although states may require parental consent for a minor's abortion when sufficient alternatives, such as judicial bypass, are in place, the same reasoning does not apply to contraception. According to the U.S. Supreme Court, "The states' interest in protection of the mental and physical health of the pregnant minor, and in protection of potential life are clearly more implicated by the abortion decision than by the decision to use a nonhazardous contraceptive" [*Carey v. Population Services International* (1977)].

Access to contraceptive services is considered a fundamental privacy right and has remained so for over three decades.

# Mandatory Reporting Laws Violate the Privacy Rights of Minors

*Sherry F. Colb*

*Sherry F. Colb is a professor of law and Charles Evans Hughes Scholar at Cornell University Law School, and she is the author of* When Sex Counts: Making Babies and Making Law.

On behalf of several health care providers and counseling services, the Center for Reproductive Rights has brought a class action lawsuit challenging the Kansas attorney general's interpretation of the state's mandatory reporting statute.

The statute requires a variety of "helping" professionals, including health care providers and educators, to report to state authorities when they have reason to suspect that a child has been injured by sexual abuse. The attorney general has taken the position that sex involving a minor is—necessarily—sexual abuse.

In support of his position, he cites the Kansas prohibition on all sexual conduct among minors under the age of 16. Accordingly, the attorney general interprets Kansas law to require professionals to report to the authorities whenever they learn that a minor has had sexual relations.

Critics of the attorney general's approach suggest that the "zero-tolerance" reading of the law is excessively broad and punitive and, significantly, denies minors their privacy.

Whether or not the Kansas trial court resolves this issue in the attorney general's favor, it will remain an important question for any state considering how to address the reality of sexual activity among minors and specifically, what role man-

Sherry F. Colb, "Should Sexually Active Minors Have a Right to Privacy? A Kansas Case Reveals the Dark Side of Mandatory Reporting," *FindLaw*, February 8, 2006. www.find law.com. Reproduced by permission.

datory reporting should play in regulating abuse. [The attorney general's interpretation was struck down by a district court in April 2006.]

## The View of Teenage Sex

In considering whether to require the reporting of teen sex, the first question is always this: What is our view of teenage sex? Many teenagers take the position that if they are old enough to reproduce, then they are old enough to have sex. Some will point out that in other cultures, both ancient and modern, people marry at a much earlier age than in the U.S., and sexual activity is a part of marriage.

Furthermore, even Kansas law allows the fact that a would-be perpetrator and victim are married to each other to stand as a defense to charges of statutory rape and aggravated indecent liberties with a child. This defense demonstrates that the law does not truly consider *all* sexual activity involving a minor to be sexual abuse.

Kansas law instead treats a teenager under 16 as *presumptively* too immature for sexual intercourse, but in at least some instances, a legal marriage is sufficient to rebut that presumption. In such cases, it is not tenable to argue that the absence of a marriage license makes the very same sexual activity between the very same people somehow "abusive."

If we accept the argument that there are individuals under the age of 16 who are emotionally and physically mature enough for sexual intercourse, then the legal prohibition against all people in this age group having sex is over-inclusive—that is, it prohibits some instances of conduct that are not, in fact, harmful.

Over-inclusiveness is not fatal to a law, but it does mean that even in a state like Kansas, where all under-16 sex is a crime, it does not follow that every sexually active teenager under 16 who visits the doctor is, by definition, an abuse victim.

If some sexually active teenagers fall outside the category of abuse victims, then a doctor or other helping professional should perhaps be allowed to use her own judgment to determine whether what has occurred truly calls for notification of the Kansas Department of Social and Rehabilitation Services.

## The Ideal-World View

One might, of course, disagree and say that in an ideal world, *no one* under the age of 16 is having sexual relations. On this view, although the law may make some (possibly inappropriate) allowances for married couples, a teenager under 16 is always too immature for responsible sexual interaction and when such interaction nonetheless occurs, a teen is almost certainly involved in an abusive and harmful relationship. One who takes this position might support the attorney general's approach.

---

*Victims of sexual abuse are as entitled to privacy as anyone else.*

---

The attorney general believes that the statute requires helping professionals who encounter sexually active teenagers to take steps that will enable the law to make the judgment it needs to make. If there is good reason to suspect abuse—and any time a minor is having sex, from this perspective, there is good reason enough—authorities should be notified.

Kansas law, as interpreted by the attorney general, simply attempts to bridge the gap between the real world and this version of the ideal world by bringing the police power to bear whenever that gap surfaces.

If we agree with the position that sex between minors is a very bad thing, does it then follow that we *should* support mandatory reporting?

## The Impact on the Victim

One could answer the question "no" for two separate reasons.

One might take the position, as some opponents of the attorney general's view have done, that mandatory reporting of minors' sexual activity violates the minors' right of privacy. Proponents respond to this suggestion that engaging in sexual abuse forfeits one's privacy.

This response, however, is truly nonresponsive. The reason for mandatory reporting is ordinarily the welfare of the minor about whom the report is being made—the *victim* of the abuse. Victims of sexual abuse are as entitled to privacy as anyone else, and their sexual victimization is hardly a ground for saying that they have forfeited that privacy.

Invoking the punitive notion of forfeiture in this context, moreover, suggests that the purpose of mandatory reporting—as construed by the attorney general—may be humiliation and prosecution rather than protection. This may also explain the attorney general's focus on abortion providers in his argument that as a matter of law, sexual abuse must necessarily have been involved in giving rise to a teen pregnancy. The desire to report all teen abortions to the authorities could well be motivated by something other than a sincere concern for the welfare of the girls involved.

To tell the authorities about a patient's or a student's sexual activity, with or without the patient's or student's willing cooperation, a doctor or teacher must betray the confidence that a minor has placed in a trusted adult. Many would consider such betrayal wrong.

Furthermore, those who share the view that teenage sex is virtually always destructive and harmful to the participants might nonetheless oppose mandatory reporting because of its impact on victims as a whole.

# The Point of Mandatory Reporting

In crafting mandatory reporting requirements, the Kansas legislature presumably had in mind the removal of an abused minor from the circumstances in which such abuse takes place. If a parent or stepparent is involved, for example, then a government caseworker could move to terminate the perpetrator's custodial or parental rights. If we extend this paradigm to include sexual interactions between two teenagers, then perhaps the authorities could take measures to keep the involved teenagers apart or to notify their parents of the need to intervene.

If we agree that intervention is desirable, though, does it therefore follow that mandatory reporting is a good idea? Not necessarily.

If health care providers and counselors consistently report teenagers' sexual activity to the authorities, teenagers might well take this policy into account when deciding whether to approach a professional in the first place. There is, in other words, an incentive problem: If Tony Teenager knows that going to the doctor will expose him to Department of Social Services intervention, he might decide not to go to the doctor at all.

If Tony makes the decision to avoid health care providers, then a number of negative consequences follow: First, if he is suffering abuse, he may become isolated in that abuse and feel unable to go to an adult to help extricate him from his circumstances; second, he might contract and ultimately spread sexually transmitted diseases (STDs) or impregnate girls, because he does not want to be reported to the authorities when he attempts to obtain contraceptives or treatment for an STD.

These consequences would qualify as disastrous by most lights.

# More Harm than Good

If one views sexual activity among minors as relatively harmless or trivial—and accordingly rejects the expansive definition of "sexual abuse" embraced by the Kansas attorney general—then the issue is easy: Do not report teenage sex. There is no good reason to do so: It compromises privacy, and it leads to terrible results. But if one honestly views teenage sex as a serious harm for the teens involved, then the issue becomes much more difficult.

---

*Mandatory reporting statutes—even when they are applied to seriously abusive circumstances—can potentially do more harm than good.*

---

Just to step into that mind-set for a moment, imagine that what we are talking about is a pediatrician discovering that a teenager has been raped by a parent. The teenager begs the pediatrician not to reveal the information to anyone, but the pediatrician worries that the abuse will continue unless she steps in. The teenager's privacy interests point in one direction, while his interest in safety and the termination of the abuse points in another. Add to these interests the fact that other teenagers who learn that their doctors, too, will report a rape to the authorities may choose to keep their victimization to themselves.

Looking at the dilemma in this way demonstrates that mandatory reporting statutes—even when they are applied to seriously abusive circumstances—can potentially do more harm than good. This reality should play a role in the decision whether to embrace mandatory reporting statutes—however broad or narrow—as a way to deal with abuse. In the individual case, it might seem outrageously irresponsible to keep secret an ongoing molestation, but the law must consider its own impact on the run of cases and any chilling effect that mandatory disclosure might have on the very population it is meant to protect.

Mandatory reporting statutes, even at their best, thus pit the particular against the general: Do we forcibly rescue one person from harm, at the risk of frightening away fifty others from even broaching the subject with a professional?

The question, moreover, is difficult, no matter how significant the alleged abuse. But when, as in the case of teen sex, there is considerable controversy about whether the conduct is even abusive, it seems highly irresponsible to pursue the zero-tolerance approach that the Kansas attorney general has adopted.

The privacy rights of teenagers *and* the hope that fewer of them will have sex prematurely both counsel a far more nuanced approach.

# Parents Have the Right to Oversee Their Children's Health Care

*Daniel Patrick Moloney*

*Daniel Patrick Moloney is a seminarian for the Catholic Archdiocese of Boston and former senior policy analyst in the Richard and Helen DeVos Center for Religion and Civil Society at the Heritage Foundation.*

In pursuing health care reform, federal and state policy makers alike need to respect and protect parental rights and responsibilities. Currently, they are not doing so.

A 14-year-old grade school girl in Kentucky arrives at the local health clinic seeking birth control. Who should decide whether she receives it? The doctor? The girl? Or her parents? The state legislature says that the girl is not even old enough to consent to sexual activity. Yet public officials, under authorization from Congress, have written rules that allow the girl to enroll in one of a number of federal programs, and this federal law would overrule state law and prohibit the clinic from informing her parents.

Thousands of similar situations occur each year—not surreptitiously, but legally, under the authority of policies and laws, some of which have been in place for decades. In exercising this authority, government intrudes into some of our most intimate living arrangements, separating parents from children, and putting the family doctor at odds with the wishes of the parents.

As a result, the moral values of ordinary people are often replaced by those of a health care establishment composed of government bureaucrats, liberal professional organizations, in-

Daniel Patrick Moloney, "Reforming Health Care to Protect Parents' Rights," Heritage Foundation, Backgrounder, no. 2181, September 15, 2008. Reproduced by permission.

dustry lobbyists, and major hospital systems. Because they control the funding and set the health care policies, they can, and often do, preempt many Americans from making health care decisions that reflect their own values.

In the continuing debate over major reforms in federal health care policy, these moral concerns are often overshadowed by other challenges—such as controlling health care costs and providing accessible health insurance to low-income Americans. But in addressing these problems, policy makers at the state and federal level must not choose solutions that would override individuals' deeply held convictions. This is especially important in our religiously and morally pluralistic society.

## Two Approaches to Health Care

The debate over health care solutions is focused on two broad and very different approaches to comprehensive reform. One is a government-controlled insurance program, either centrally managed and regulated or based almost exclusively on government payment. The other is based on personal choice and market competition, where individuals and families make the key financial decisions, particularly when it comes to insurance coverage, benefits, medical procedures, and treatments. On the question of whose moral values are controlling the sensitive matter of health care decision making, these two approaches are worlds apart.

A national health insurance program, government-run or government-controlled, would centralize control over health care financing and delivery, and would centralize the power of approved third-party payers to impose their values on a morally pluralistic society. Political decisions would, in effect, supplant moral ones. A reform based on personal choice and competition in a pluralistic market would ensure that patients—or in the case of minors, their parents—exercise the primary control over how their health care dollars are spent, allowing them to make health care decisions that are consistent with their values. A market-based reform, in other words, is inherently compatible with parental authority.

## The Bureaucratic Suppression of Moral Decisions

Current federal health insurance programs routinely govern the health care of minors in ever larger numbers, and in so doing, government officials preempt or interfere with important decisions that should be made by parents. In contrast, new policies that would inject principles of consumer choice and competition into the financing and delivery of health care can restore respect for the primary relationships between parents and children, leaving families free to live according to their moral convictions.

*Federal laws and the reigning ethos of the professional health care associations intrude on intimate health care choices of parents and families.*

To better understand how government currently intrudes on these relationships, consider again the 14-year-old girl in Kentucky requesting birth control at a health clinic. Examine further the details from this real-life case:

> The girl told the doctor that she was not yet sexually active, but that the mother of her boyfriend, who had driven her to the clinic, wanted her on birth control so that her son would not father a child out of wedlock if they were to have sex. The girl wants her boyfriend to like her, she told the doctor, and she wanted to remain on good terms with his mother. That's why she was asking to be put on prescription birth control. However, she does not want her parents to find out. Because the girl requested confidentiality, the doctor had her enroll in a federal program to pay for the contraception, so that the charges would not show up on her parents' insurance bill.

Unless they pay close attention to the health care debates in state legislatures, typical Americans are unaware of the intrusiveness of current government policy. Representatives of professional health care organizations often argue that minors should be allowed to receive reproductive health care without their parents' knowledge or consent. The American Academy of Pediatrics states bluntly, "Comprehensive health care of adolescents should include a sexual history that should be obtained in a safe, nonthreatening environment through open, honest, and nonjudgmental communication, with assurances of confidentiality. . . . The primary reason adolescents hesitate or delay obtaining family planning or contraceptive services is concern about confidentiality." Specifically for this reason, Congress enacted a federal law, popularly known as Title X [Family Planning program], which provides that whenever a sexually active minor seeks confidential birth control, she is to be treated independently from her parents. Therefore, she can accept birth control without consulting her parents, and if she requests confidentiality without parental knowledge, the government will foot the bill for her contraception and related medical costs, regardless of her parents' income.

Under current law, Congress makes confidential access to birth control for school-age girls such a priority that it picks up the tab even for services that the girl's family insurance would cover. Since federal law trumps state law, it does not matter that the laws of her state deem her too young to consent to sex.

## Two Real Cases

*Limiting Medical Judgment.* Doctors make delicate decisions about teen health care every day, but current federal confidentiality rules can render it nearly impossible for a doctor to perform the medical action that his professional judgment demands. Consider, for example, the case of the 16-year-old boy in North Carolina who went to his pediatrician complaining of severe daily headaches. The doctor questioned the boy after his mother stepped out of the room, and discovered that the boy regularly used marijuana and cocaine, and occasionally LSD, hallucinogenic mushrooms, and ecstasy. The doctor informed the boy that his headaches might be related to his drug use, and recommended that he undergo treatment for substance abuse. The doctor asked for permission to tell his mother, and the boy said no. He said he was not afraid of his parents' reaction; he simply thought he had his drug use under control, it was no big deal, and his parents would not care. Under North Carolina law, if the child is on private insurance and the doctor judges the matter "essential to the life or health of a minor," he can ignore the boy's request for confidentiality and tell the mother about his addiction. In this case, the doctor did tell the mother, and the boy was enrolled in a drug treatment program a few weeks later.

---

*Parents have the primary responsibility for their children, and thus ought to play a paramount role in any decisions affecting their children's lives.*

---

*The Medicaid Angle.* If the child's family had been on Medicaid instead of private insurance, the story would have been different. Under federal law, Medicaid prohibits any doctor from breaching the confidentiality of any patient, even to the parents of children. Had the boy's family been enrolled in Medicaid, the law would have enforced his right to confidential medical care, deferring to the short-term self-interest of a drug-addicted minor and overruling the doctor's expert judgment regarding his objective medical needs.

In both of these real cases, federal laws and the reigning ethos of the professional health care associations intrude on intimate health care choices of parents and families. In both cases, they exclude parents from key decisions regarding the welfare of their own children. In both cases, they impose one set of values on the entire country, trampling on local and state laws reflecting their communities' deliberate moral judgments.

## Government Health Programs Separate Parents and Children

Problems of parental choice and control are typical in federal health care programs, especially in Medicaid, SCHIP [State Children's Health Insurance Program], and Title X.

*Medicaid.* Medicaid, for instance, prohibits parental notification for any medical procedure it covers. This means that children are not required to notify their parents if, while on Medicaid, they receive any of the following medical services (this list is not exhaustive):

- abortions (in the cases of rape, incest, and the life of the mother),

- birth control,

- pregnancy tests,

- the morning-after pill,

- tests for sexually transmitted diseases,

- gynecological exams,

- prescription drugs,

- treatment for drug abuse,

- treatment for psychiatric disorders (including depression, suicide, and attention deficit disorder),

- sexual orientation counseling, and

- personalized sexual education.

As in the example of the drug-using teenager above, the doctor is prohibited from informing the parent of a child on

Medicaid about the case, even if the doctor believes it is in the best interests of the child, unless he can obtain the consent of the minor.

*SCHIP.* Medicaid is a welfare program. While children of working and middle-class families are not eligible for Medicaid, they are often eligible for another federal program called the State Children's Health Insurance Program (SCHIP). In a number of states, however, this program is an extension of Medicaid and offers many of the same services—including abortion, birth control, psychiatric treatment, substance abuse treatment, prescription drugs, and sex education—but specifically for children.

Under SCHIP each state can elect to apply Medicaid's rules, or to design an entirely different program from scratch. Despite this flexibility, however, all 50 states continue to offer Medicaid-style family planning services for children, and most states have also continued Medicaid's policies regarding confidential care for minors. As a result, children from middle-class families are frequently able to receive these services without their parents' knowledge.

*Title X.* In addition to Medicaid and SCHIP, which pay for a full range of medical care, the federal government also has a special program that funds only reproductive health care and activities related to population control, the above-mentioned Title X. Under Title X, a clinic charges its clients based on their ability to pay for its services, from wealthy clients who pay full price to lower-income patients who pay a nominal fee or nothing at all.

## Confidentiality Rules

While Medicaid and SCHIP only pay for children who qualify for their programs, the Title X program will completely cover confidential birth control for any child who is not independently wealthy. Once a girl asks that her parents not be notified, as in the case of the 14-year-old Kentucky girl, the government pays for her services, which include birth control, the morning-after pill, gynecological examinations, and abortion. The Guttmacher Institute, the research arm of Planned Parenthood, says that Title X is the "gold standard" of teen confidentiality rules, and it lobbies federal and state lawmakers to incorporate these rules into every expansion of government control over health insurance.

Because Title X confidentiality rules are so strong and apply to children, clinics supported by the program can even facilitate statutory rape, whereby adult men molest minor girls. In January of 1996, a 13-year-old girl went to a McHenry County health clinic in Illinois to request Depo-Provera, a long-term contraceptive injection. She told the doctor that she was sexually active and that she did not want her parents to know, so she received confidential services just like the 14-year-old Kentucky girl. After she received a prescription for the injection, her sex partner—her 37-year-old former teacher at Crystal Lake Middle School—drove her home from the clinic. They returned for follow-up shots on multiple occasions before she finally told her parents in February 1997. More than two years later, when the parents tried to sue the clinic for facilitating statutory rape, a county judge ruled that the doctor's actions were legal under Title X.

---

*Parents have a right to pass on their moral values to their children.*

---

Finally, parents should be aware that health clinics based in public schools receive funds from all three of these federal programs, and therefore are often governed by their rules prohibiting parental access to their children's health records. Nearly three-quarters of school-based clinics receive funds from Medicaid, and over half also receive funds from SCHIP. Many of these clinics receive Title X funds themselves or have contracts with Title X clinics to provide reproductive services and sex education programs. In a school-based clinic that receives Title X funds, for example, a wealthy minor on private insurance can, at the discretion of the doctor, enroll in a government program that permits confidential access to birth control, STD [sexually transmitted disease] testing, abortion, and more. Indeed, the movement toward including more elaborate clinics in public schools was in part to ensure that teenagers had access to confidential birth control.

## The Need to Return Power to Parents

Parents have the primary responsibility for their children, and thus ought to play a paramount role in any decisions affecting their children's lives. Doctors and government officials should certainly be allowed to contribute their professional advice or financial support, but the parents must have the ultimate right, in all but extraordinary circumstances, to raise their children the way they deem best. Medicaid, SCHIP, Title X, and other government health insurance programs routinely violate this most basic of principles. Members of Congress and state legislators alike should, therefore, take decisive steps to reform all three programs.

*Obstacles to Change.* Reform-minded legislators must be prepared, however, to overcome certain obstacles. Poorer parents often have no choice but to enroll in a government program such as Medicaid or SCHIP, and so are at the mercy of the health care establishment that sets the rules for the program. Because the government provides their health care, it determines the requirements to remain eligible—and the result is that it removes the right of the parent to make many of the key moral decisions that are only the parents' responsibility. Parents' only practical alternative is to accept those rules or not have any health insurance at all. If parents had the ability to choose from a variety of health care options, they could walk away from a situation in which they were not happy and seek better treatment elsewhere.

Most people receive their health insurance through the government or their employer, and do not have the personal power to change insurance companies except at a very high cost. As a result, insurance companies, hospitals, and doctors are not required to be as responsive to the demands of the patients as are suppliers of other goods and services in a normally functioning competitive economy. If more Americans controlled their own health insurance, and could easily switch insurance companies whenever a better health plan became available, the entire health care sector of the economy would become much friendlier to consumers and patients. Greater personal control over health care dollars, including where to purchase health insurance and from whom, would lead to a health care system far more responsive to people's needs than it is today—including their wish to have their deeply held moral views respected in the financing and delivery of care.

## The Rights of Parents

*Key Principles of Sound Reform.* Any reform that gives parents control over the health care decisions for their families should be based on four principles:

1. Individual patients, not employers or government bureaucrats, should be able to choose their health insurance coverage for themselves and their families.

2. Each person must be able to change insurance companies easily, without requiring an employment change or suffering major tax or regulatory penalties as in effect today.

3. Each person should have a variety of insurance plans from which to choose, including health plans that reflect different life situations and respect individual values.

4. Americans should be given ownership of their health insurance coverage so that an unaccountable third party does not have control over its contents and quality—and the values it embodies.

*Parental Values.* Parents have the right to pass on their moral values to their children. That right is often disregarded in the regular course of financing and delivering medical services.

The disconnect between personal values, particularly traditional moral beliefs, and the reigning ethos is no more clearly demonstrated than in today's government-controlled health care programs. In these programs, the ethos governing health care reflects the values of the bureaucrats, professional organizations, industry lobbyists, and the administrators of big hospitals that embody the health care establishment.

Generally speaking, the representatives of these groups share a commitment to allowing children to receive sexual and mental health services without their parents' knowledge, consent, or involvement. While they may publicly warn legislators not to impose traditional moral values in the formulation or execution of public policy, they see no contradiction in the forcible imposition of their own moral perspectives throughout the health care system in every state in the country, overriding state laws and the protection of parents' rights. They can do this because the government programs that they control and influence are, practically speaking, the only health care options for many people.

## Restoring Parents' Rights

The experience with Medicaid, SCHIP, Title X, and other government-funded health insurance programs illustrates the adage, "He who pays the piper, calls the tune." If someone other than the patient controls how the doctor is paid, someone other than the patient controls the moral decisions embodied in the financing and delivery of care.

For this reason, broad health care reform cannot simply tinker with the current system in which employers and government officials retain the key levers of control. A federally administered national health insurance plan, based on a set of moral values determined by "experts," would be particularly threatening to parents, families, and all those who do not share the moral values of the health care establishment or of the reigning political party.

Parents have the primary responsibility for the welfare of their children, and policy makers must respect their right to make decisions for their children. A central goal of any health care reform, therefore, must be to allow parents to own and control their family's health insurance. This would allow them to make key moral decisions that affect their children, restoring them to the role that is naturally and rightfully theirs.

# Parents Have a Right to Know About Teen Abortion

*Mailee R. Smith*

*Mailee R. Smith is staff counsel at Americans United for Life, a national pro-life organization.*

Thirteen-year-old "Jane Doe" was your everyday teen: She attended school and played on the school soccer team. But her normal life turned into a nightmare when her soccer coach initiated a sexual relationship with her, impregnated her, and took her to a local Ohio Planned Parenthood clinic for an abortion. The clinic never questioned the soccer coach, who posed over the phone as Jane's father and then personally paid for the girl's abortion. And where were her real parents? Their true consent was never sought. In fact, they were never even informed.

Sadly, Jane's story is not unique. Almost daily, news stories reveal yet another teen that has been sexually abused by a person in authority—be it a coach, teacher, or other authority figure. Daily, teens are taken to abortion clinics without the consent or even the knowledge of their parents. The health and welfare of these minors is at risk in every state in which parental involvement laws have not been enacted.

## The Constitutionality of Parental Involvement Laws

In 1992, a plurality of the United States Supreme Court (USSC) ruled that a state may constitutionally require a minor seeking an abortion to obtain the consent of a parent or guardian. Specifically, the USSC held that certain provisions, such as a required reflection period and a chance for parents

Mailee R. Smith, "Parental Involvement Laws: Protecting Minors and Parental Rights," *Defending Life 2009*, Americans United for Life, 2009, pp. 177–179. Reproduced by permission.

to privately discuss with their daughters the values and moral principles in the situation, carry particular force with respect to minors. Based upon the Court's decision and subsequent lower federal court decisions, a parental involvement law is constitutional and does not place an undue burden on minors if it contains the following provisions:

- No physician may perform an abortion upon a minor or incompetent person unless the physician performing the abortion has received the consent of one parent or legal guardian (parental consent) or given 48 hours notice to one parent or the legal guardian of the minor or incompetent person (parental notice).

- An exception to the requirement exists when there is a medical emergency or, in the case of parental notice, when notice is waived by the person entitled to such notice.

- A minor may bypass the requirement through the courts (*i.e.*, judicial bypass).

## The Purpose of Parental Involvement Laws

The purpose behind parental involvement laws is clear. Immature minors often lack the ability to make fully informed choices that take into account both immediate and long-range consequences. Yet the medical, emotional, and psychological consequences of abortion are often serious and can be lasting, particularly when the patient is immature. Moreover, parents usually possess information essential to a physician's exercise of his or her best medical judgment concerning the minor. Parents who are aware that their daughter has had an abortion may better ensure the best post-abortion medical attention. As such, parental consultation is usually desirable and in the best interest of the minor. For these reasons, parental involvement laws protect the health and welfare of minors as well as foster family unity and protect the constitutional rights of parents to rear their children. . . .

## Myths About Parental Involvement Laws

*Myth*: An estimated 12 percent of teens do not even live with their parents. Notifying the parents of these teens will be impossible and totally unrelated to the teen's health.

*Fact*: Parental involvement legislation recognizes that many family situations are less than ideal. In most states, alternative procedures are available through judicial bypass, and some states allow notification or consent of another family member.

*Myth*: Mandatory parental involvement and notification laws will force many teens to go out of state to obtain an abortion.

*Fact*: As more states enact and enforce parental involvement laws, the option to go out of state will cease to exist, and parental rights and minors' health protection will continue to expand. Migration to other states is a reason to pass parental involvement laws, not to avoid them.

*Myth*: Parental involvement laws simply delay teens from getting abortions until the second trimester, when abortion is more dangerous.

*Fact*: This myth is directly contrary to data from both Minnesota and Missouri.

*Myth*: Parental involvement laws force teens to obtain dangerous illegal abortions.

*Fact*: The majority of states have working parental involvement laws. Only one case—that of Becky Bell in Indiana—has been suggested to involve an unsafe abortion, and even that case is wholly undocumented. The autopsy report failed to show an induced abortion. It is terrible public policy to fail to enact a law on the basis of an isolated, unproven case.

*Myth*: Parental involvement laws expose teens to the anger of abusive parents.

*Fact*: Under the parental involvement laws in most states, a teen who states that she has been abused or neglected will be exempted from the applicable law's requirements. In addition, such laws make it more likely that a minor who is being abused or neglected will get the help she needs; under most state laws, doctors who become aware of abuse claims must report the abuse allegation to public officials who conduct an anonymous investigation. Such teens also have the option of utilizing the judicial bypass procedure.

*Myth*: Most teens are mature enough to make their own decisions.

*Fact*: Young teens often have difficulty assessing long-term consequences and generally have narrow and egocentric views of their problems. Parental involvement is needed to give teenagers some perspective. Moreover, the question is not simply of maturity, but of responsibility. As long as a teenager is not emancipated, a parent is responsible for her medical care and upbringing. When a teen is injured by an abortion, it is the parent—not the teen—who is responsible for the teen's care and health costs.

# Contraceptives Should Not Be Available to Young Teens Without Parental Consent

**Patriot Ledger**

*The* Patriot Ledger *is a daily newspaper that serves communities south of Boston, Massachusetts.*

Yes, children should be taught sexual responsibility and, yes, we should be giving them all the tools we can to help them make what could be life-changing decisions when it comes to sex.

## An Abdication of Parental Responsibility

But, good grief, even the most liberal among us should recoil at the decision by school officials in Portland, Maine, to dispense birth control pills and other contraceptive medications to middle school students—11-, 12-, and 13-year-olds—without parental consent.

No matter how those on Portland's school committee who voted for this dangerous decision rationalize their actions, it is a total abdication of responsibility and admission of defeat and please spare us the excuse that some kids will be doing it anyway.

There are those who use religion as the basis for their opposition while others claim a move such as this unfairly excises parental rights.

We think more to the point is this decision lets irresponsible parents unable to talk to their children off scot-free. They can now sleep comfortably believing their daughter will not become a teen mother.

*Patriot Ledger* (Quincy, MA), "There Has to Be a Limit," October 19, 2007, p. 6. Reprinted by permission.

But handing out pills and patches to little girls—and that is what they are—is frightening in the message it relays as to how we want them to think about their bodies and themselves.

## Reasonable Fears About Access to Contraception

In [a] way, we are buying into that argument that fuller access to birth control can promote promiscuity. But at that age, when children are at their most susceptible to peer pressure and a yearning to grow up too fast, too soon, is it not a reasonable fear?

Can we expect a 12-year-old to use a condom that could protect her from a sexually transmitted disease when she knows the birth control pill is more effective against unwanted pregnancy?

Can we trust an 11-year-old child to not want to experiment in becoming a grown-up when we are giving her access to adult medications that she can choose to tell her parents about or not?

Can young girls be expected to weigh the long-term effects of chemically manipulated estrogen and hormonal levels, clotting risks and possible cancer from some of the forms of birth control?

And this action in no way holds boys responsible for their actions or teaches them accountability for their part in this sexual tango.

We have always favored more rather than less information for teenagers to make educated decisions when it comes to sex. While abstinence-only has a place in sex education, it is naive to think some, even many, youngsters will not engage in sexual activity before they turn 18.

There is an argument that some parents are too timid or too much in denial to talk with their tweens [preteens] about sex. That, though, should not mean their children should suffer because of their inability to be a parent.

What seems to be lost in all of this is that these girls are not even at the age of consent. Anyone who has sex with them is committing child rape.

Do we really want to encourage that?

# CHAPTER 3

# Should Teens Have Privacy Rights Respected at School?

# Overview: Teen Privacy Rights and Drug Testing at School

*Students for Sensible Drug Policy*

*Students for Sensible Drug Policy is an international network of students who are concerned about the impact of drug abuse but who believe that the war on drugs is failing society.*

While proponents of [drug] testing claim that it keeps teens away from drugs, research shows that the practice fails to reduce youth drug use and can actually make existing school drug problems worse. Drug testing students is also very expensive and invasive.

## The Problems with Student Drug Testing

A 2003 study funded by the National Institute on Drug Abuse [NIDA]—the largest of its kind—examined 94,000 students at 900 schools in the U.S. and found no difference between levels of drug use at schools that test their students and those that do not. The study concluded, "[S]chool drug testing was not associated with either the prevalence or frequency of student marijuana use, or of other illicit drug use." Dr. Lloyd Johnston, one of the three University of Michigan researchers who conducted the study, commented, "[Drug testing is] the kind of intervention that doesn't win the hearts and minds of children. I don't think it brings about any constructive changes in their attitudes about drugs or their belief in the dangers associated with using them."

In addition to being ineffective, there is evidence suggesting drug testing actually exacerbates the problem of teen drug abuse. Because most schools that test do so as a condition of participating in extracurricular activities, at-risk students may

Students for Sensible Drug Policy, "Eliminate the Harmful and Costly Student Drug Testing Grants," 2007. www.ssdp.org. Reproduced by permission.

be deterred from getting involved in such activities rather than from using drugs. Research shows that teen drug use and other dangerous behavior is highest between 3:00 and 6:00 p.m.—the unsupervised hours between the end of the school day and the time parents get home from work. As a result, those who choose not to submit to drug tests sacrifice extracurricular involvement and are at greater risk of abusing drugs or engaging in other dangerous behavior. According to Dr. Howard Taras, chair of the American Academy of Pediatrics Council on School Health, "[Drug testing] may decrease involvement in extracurricular activities among students who regularly use or have once used drugs. Without engagement in healthy activities, adolescents are more likely to drop out of school, become pregnant, join gangs, pursue substance abuse and engage in other risky behaviors."

In addition, students may turn to more dangerous but less detectable drugs in order to avoid testing positive. Reasoning that marijuana is the most detectable drug, students may be driven to use other "harder" drugs, like meth [methamphetamine], ecstasy, inhalants, or cocaine, which are far less detectable. False positives—when drug tests erroneously reveal drug use in students who have not used drugs—are relatively common, leading to the improper punishment of innocent students.

---

*Random suspicionless testing poisons important relationships of trust between students and educators.*

---

With costs ranging between $10 and $75 per test, it is unconscionable for federal dollars to be earmarked for a program of questionable effectiveness while schools struggle to adequately pay teachers and fund valuable extracurricular programs. One school in Dublin, Ohio, for example, canceled its $35,000 per year drug testing program after determining it was not cost effective. Of 1,473 students tested at $24 each, 11 tested positive, for a total cost of $3,200 per "positive" student. After canceling the program, the school used the savings to hire a full-time counselor and provided prevention programs that reached all 3,581 students.

## The Invasiveness of Drug Testing

Many schools that drug test require students to produce urine samples while school officials stand outside the door listening for the sounds of urination to guard against tampered specimens. In addition to putting school officials at risk of being sued for sexual assault, this is invasive and embarrassing for students, and sends the message that they are guilty until proven innocent. Students need to know that they can go to school officials for help if they have problems with drugs, but random suspicionless testing poisons important relationships of trust between students and educators and makes it less likely that alienated adolescents will seek help when they need it.

In the event of positive test results, schools often ask students to provide lists of prescription and over-the-counter medications they are taking in order to ascertain whether or not those drugs may have produced a false positive. This means that students taking birth control or antidepressants may be forced to disclose this information to school officials.

According to the 2003 NIDA study, 95 percent of American schools do not randomly drug test their student athletes, and only two percent of schools randomly test students who participate in extracurriculars other than athletics. Prominent organizations that oppose random suspicionless student drug testing include the National Education Association, the Association for Addiction Professionals, the American Public Health Association, the American Academy of Pediatrics, the National Association of Social Workers, and the National Council on Alcoholism and Drug Dependence.

## The Legal Status of Student Drug Testing

While the Supreme Court narrowly ruled (by a 5–4 margin) in 2002 that schools can require students involved in competitive extracurricular activities to submit to drug tests, it is important to note that the Court's ruling on the constitutionality of student drug testing only interpreted federal law. Many state laws and constitutions provide additional protections for student privacy. In fact, lawsuits have been filed against school districts in several states over their student drug testing policies. This means that schools electing to drug test their students are subject to tremendous legal liability. Laws vary greatly from state to state, and in the absence of state court decisions upholding drug testing, school districts run the serious risk of financial ruin in the event of a lawsuit, even when successfully defended. Even in cases where drug testing is legally permissible, the mere appearance of mishandling sensitive medical information or misconduct in administering the tests can invite litigation. This increases the actual cost of drug testing programs due to the need to hire attorneys to ensure legal compliance and to purchase tort insurance to protect against potential lawsuits.

In 2006, ONDCP/DOE [Office of National Drug Control Policy/Department of Education] granted money to 66 school districts with 362 schools, each grant averaging approximately $125,000. The schools must include in the random testing pool all students who participate in athletic programs and/or all who are engaged in competitive extracurricular school-sponsored activities.

There are many deserving programs that are underfunded, yet are actually effective at keeping teens healthy and out of trouble.

# Students Have Rights Preventing Schools from Conducting Unwarranted Searches

*David Souter*

*David Souter was associate justice of the US Supreme Court from 1990 until his retirement in 2009. He was appointed to the Court by President George H.W. Bush.*

The issue here is whether a 13-year-old student's Fourth Amendment right was violated when she was subjected to a search of her bra and underpants by school officials acting on reasonable suspicion that she had brought forbidden prescription and over-the-counter drugs to school. Because there were no reasons to suspect the drugs presented a danger or were concealed in her underwear, we hold that the search did violate the Constitution, but because there is reason to question the clarity with which the right was established, the official who ordered the unconstitutional search is entitled to qualified immunity from liability.

## A Student Search

The events immediately prior to the search in question began in 13-year-old Savana Redding's math class at Safford Middle School one October day in 2003. The assistant principal of the school, Kerry Wilson, came into the room and asked Savana to go to his office. There, he showed her a day planner, unzipped and open flat on his desk, in which there were several knives, lighters, a permanent marker, and a cigarette. Wilson asked Savana whether the planner was hers; she said it was,

David Souter, *Safford Unified School District #1 v. April Redding*, June 25, 2009.

but that a few days before she had lent it to her friend, Marissa Glines. Savana stated that none of the items in the planner belonged to her.

Wilson then showed Savana four white prescription strength ibuprofen 400-mg [milligram] pills, and one over-the-counter blue naproxen 200-mg pill, all used for pain and inflammation but banned under school rules without advance permission. He asked Savana if she knew anything about the pills. Savana answered that she did not. Wilson then told Savana that he had received a report that she was giving these pills to fellow students; Savana denied it and agreed to let Wilson search her belongings. Helen Romero, an administrative assistant, came into the office, and together with Wilson they searched Savana's backpack, finding nothing.

At that point, Wilson instructed Romero to take Savana to the school nurse's office to search her clothes for pills. Romero and the nurse, Peggy Schwallier, asked Savana to remove her jacket, socks, and shoes, leaving her in stretch pants and a T-shirt (both without pockets), which she was then asked to remove. Finally, Savana was told to pull her bra out to the side and shake it, and to pull out the elastic on her underpants, thus exposing her breasts and pelvic area to some degree. No pills were found.

## An Allegation of a Fourth Amendment Violation

Savana's mother filed suit against Safford Unified School District #1, Wilson, Romero, and Schwallier for conducting a strip search in violation of Savana's Fourth Amendment rights. The individuals (hereinafter petitioners) moved for summary judgment, raising a defense of qualified immunity. The District Court for the District of Arizona granted the motion on the ground that there was no Fourth Amendment violation, and a panel of the Ninth Circuit affirmed.

A closely divided Circuit sitting en banc [with all judges], however, reversed. Following the two-step protocol for evaluating claims of qualified immunity, the Ninth Circuit held that the strip search was unjustified under the Fourth Amendment test for searches of children by school officials set out in *New Jersey v. T.L.O.* (1985). The Circuit then applied the test for qualified immunity, and found that Savana's right was clearly established at the time of the search: "[t]hese notions of personal privacy are 'clearly established' in that they inhere in all of us, particularly middle school teenagers, and are inherent in the privacy component of the Fourth Amendment's proscription against unreasonable searches." . . .

---

*The lesser standard for school searches could as readily be described as a moderate chance of finding evidence of wrongdoing.*

---

The Fourth Amendment "right of the people to be secure in their persons . . . against unreasonable searches and seizures" generally requires a law enforcement officer to have probable cause for conducting a search. "Probable cause exists where 'the facts and circumstances within [an officer's] knowledge and of which [he] had reasonably trustworthy information [are] sufficient in themselves to warrant a man of reasonable caution in the belief that' an offense has been or is being committed" [*Brinegar v. United States* (1949) (quoting *Carroll v. United States* [1925])], and that evidence bearing on that offense will be found in the place to be searched.

In *T.L.O.*, we recognized that the school setting "requires some modification of the level of suspicion of illicit activity needed to justify a search," and held that for searches by school officials "a careful balancing of governmental and private interests suggests that the public interest is best served by a Fourth Amendment standard of reasonableness that stops short of probable cause." We have thus applied a standard of reasonable suspicion to determine the legality of a school administrator's search of a student, and have held that a school search "will be permissible in its scope when the measures adopted are reasonably related to the objectives of the search and not excessively intrusive in light of the age and sex of the student and the nature of the infraction."

A number of our cases on probable cause have an implicit bearing on the reliable knowledge element of reasonable suspicion, as we have attempted to flesh out the knowledge component by looking to the degree to which known facts imply prohibited conduct, the specificity of the information received, and the reliability of its source. At the end of the day, however, we have realized that these factors cannot rigidly control, and we have come back to saying that the standards are "fluid concepts that take their substantive content from the particular contexts" in which they are being assessed [*Ornelas v. United States* (1996)].

Perhaps the best that can be said generally about the required knowledge component of probable cause for a law enforcement officer's evidence search is that it raise a "fair probability," or a "substantial chance" [*Illinois v. Gates* (1983)], of discovering evidence of criminal activity. The lesser standard for school searches could as readily be described as a moderate chance of finding evidence of wrongdoing.

## A School's Concern About Drugs

In this case, the school's policies strictly prohibit the non-medical use, possession, or sale of any drug on school grounds, including "'[a]ny prescription or over-the-counter drug, except those for which permission to use in school has been granted pursuant to Board policy.'" A week before Savana was searched, another student, Jordan Romero (no relation of the school's administrative assistant), told the principal and Assistant Principal Wilson that "certain students were bringing drugs and weapons on campus," and that he had been sick after taking some pills that "he got from a classmate." On the morning of October 8, the same boy handed Wilson a white pill that he said Marissa Glines had given him. He told Wilson that students were planning to take the pills at lunch.

Wilson learned from Peggy Schwallier, the school nurse, that the pill was ibuprofen 400 mg, available only by prescription. Wilson then called Marissa out of class. Outside the classroom, Marissa's teacher handed Wilson the day planner, found within Marissa's reach, containing various contraband items. Wilson escorted Marissa back to his office.

In the presence of Helen Romero, Wilson requested Marissa to turn out her pockets and open her wallet. Marissa produced a blue pill, several white ones, and a razor blade. Wilson asked where the blue pill came from, and Marissa answered, "'I guess it slipped in when *she* gave me the IBU 400s.'" When Wilson asked whom she meant, Marissa replied, "'Savana Redding.'" Wilson then enquired about the day planner and its contents; Marissa denied knowing anything about them. Wilson did not ask Marissa any follow-up questions to determine whether there was any likelihood that Savana presently had pills: neither asking when Marissa received the pills from Savana nor where Savana might be hiding them.

---

*This suspicion of Wilson's was enough to justify a search of Savana's backpack and outer clothing.*

---

Schwallier did not immediately recognize the blue pill, but information provided through a poison control hotline indicated that the pill was a 200-mg dose of an anti-inflammatory drug, generically called naproxen, available over the counter. At Wilson's direction, Marissa was then subjected to a search of her bra and underpants by Romero and Schwallier, as Savana was later on. The search revealed no additional pills.

## A Justified Search

It was at this juncture that Wilson called Savana into his office and showed her the day planner. Their conversation established that Savana and Marissa were on friendly terms: While she denied knowledge of the contraband, Savana admitted that the day planner was hers and that she had lent it to Marissa. Wilson had other reports of their friendship from staff members, who had identified Savana and Marissa as part of an unusually rowdy group at the school's opening dance in August, during which alcohol and cigarettes were found in the girls' bathroom. Wilson had reason to connect the girls with this contraband, for Wilson knew that Jordan Romero had told the principal that before the dance, he had been at a party at Savana's house where alcohol was served. Marissa's statement that the pills came from Savana was thus sufficiently plausible to warrant suspicion that Savana was involved in pill distribution.

This suspicion of Wilson's was enough to justify a search of Savana's backpack and outer clothing. If a student is reasonably suspected of giving out contraband pills, she is reasonably suspected of carrying them on her person and in the carryall that has become an item of student uniform in most places today. If Wilson's reasonable suspicion of pill distribution were not understood to support searches of outer clothes and backpack, it would not justify any search worth making. And the look into Savana's bag, in her presence and in the relative privacy of Wilson's office, was not excessively intrusive, any more than Romero's subsequent search of her outer clothing.

## A Reasonable Expectation of Privacy

Here it is that the parties part company, with Savana's claim that extending the search at Wilson's behest to the point of making her pull out her underwear was constitutionally unreasonable. The exact label for this final step in the intrusion is not important, though strip search is a fair way to speak of it. Romero and Schwallier directed Savana to remove her clothes down to her underwear, and then "pull out" her bra and the elastic band on her underpants. Although Romero and Schwallier stated that they did not see anything when Savana followed their instructions, we would not define strip search and its Fourth Amendment consequences in a way that would guarantee litigation about who was looking and how much was seen. The very fact of Savana's pulling her underwear away from her body in the presence of the two officials who were able to see her necessarily exposed breasts and pelvic area to some degree, and both subjective and reasonable societal expectations of personal privacy support the treatment of such a search as categorically distinct, requiring distinct elements of justification on the part of school authorities for going beyond a search of outer clothing and belongings.

---

*The content of the suspicion failed to match the degree of intrusion.*

---

Savana's subjective expectation of privacy against such a search is inherent in her account of it as embarrassing, frightening, and humiliating. The reasonableness of her expectation (required by the Fourth Amendment standard) is indicated by the consistent experiences of other young people similarly searched, whose adolescent vulnerability intensifies the patent intrusiveness of the exposure. The common reaction of these adolescents simply registers the obviously different meaning of a search exposing the body from the experience of nakedness or near undress in other school circumstances. Changing for gym is getting ready for play; exposing for a search is responding to an accusation reserved for suspected wrongdoers and fairly understood as so degrading that a number of communities have decided that strip searches in schools are never reasonable and have banned them no matter what the facts may be.

The indignity of the search does not, of course, outlaw it, but it does implicate the rule of reasonableness as stated in *T.L.O.*, that "the search as actually conducted [be] reasonably related in scope to the circumstances which justified the interference in the first place." The scope will be permissible, that is, when it is "not excessively intrusive in light of the age and sex of the student and the nature of the infraction."

## An Unreasonable Search

Here, the content of the suspicion failed to match the degree of intrusion. Wilson knew beforehand that the pills were prescription-strength ibuprofen and over-the-counter naproxen, common pain relievers equivalent to two Advil, or one Aleve. He must have been aware of the nature and limited threat of the specific drugs he was searching for, and while just about anything can be taken in quantities that will do real harm, Wilson had no reason to suspect that large amounts of the drugs were being passed around, or that individual students were receiving great numbers of pills.

Nor could Wilson have suspected that Savana was hiding common painkillers in her underwear. Petitioners suggest, as a truth universally acknowledged, that "students . . . hid[e] contraband in or under their clothing," and cite a smattering of cases of students with contraband in their underwear. But when the categorically extreme intrusiveness of a search down to the body of an adolescent requires some justification in suspected facts, general background possibilities fall short; a reasonable search that extensive calls for suspicion that it will pay off. But nondangerous school contraband does not raise the specter of stashes in intimate places, and there is no evidence in the record of any general practice among Safford Middle School students of hiding that sort of thing in underwear; neither Jordan nor Marissa suggested to Wilson that Savana was doing that, and the preceding search of Marissa that Wilson ordered yielded nothing. Wilson never even determined when Marissa had received the pills from Savana; if it had been a few days before, that would weigh heavily against any reasonable conclusion that Savana presently had the pills on her person, much less in her underwear.

In sum, what was missing from the suspected facts that pointed to Savana was any indication of danger to the students from the power of the drugs or their quantity, and any reason to suppose that Savana was carrying pills in her underwear. We think that the combination of these deficiencies was fatal to finding the search reasonable.

## The Limits of School Searches

In so holding, we mean to cast no ill reflection on the assistant principal, for the record raises no doubt that his motive throughout was to eliminate drugs from his school and protect students from what Jordan Romero had gone through. Parents are known to overreact to protect their children from danger, and a school official with responsibility for safety may tend to do the same. The difference is that the Fourth Amendment places limits on the official, even with the high degree of deference that courts must pay to the educator's professional judgment.

We do mean, though, to make it clear that the *T.L.O.* concern to limit a school search to reasonable scope requires the support of reasonable suspicion of danger or of resort to underwear for hiding evidence of wrongdoing before a search can reasonably make the quantum leap from outer clothes and backpacks to exposure of intimate parts. The meaning of such a search, and the degradation its subject may reasonably feel, place a search that intrusive in a category of its own, demanding its own specific suspicions. . . .

The strip search of Savana Redding was unreasonable and a violation of the Fourth Amendment.

# Schools Should Not Interfere with Student Speech off Campus

*Justin Silverman*

*Justin Silverman is a law student at Suffolk University Law School and interned at the Citizen Media Law Project.*

A freshman at Oak Grove High School in Missouri used Facebook last month [February 2010] to vent about another student: "Wow, [expletive] alert," wrote Megan Wisemore. "You're a skank and I hate you with a [expletive] passion." Though Wisemore intended only for her friends to see the message, the classmate she wrote about eventually read the posting as well. When Wisemore returned to school, that classmate attacked her in retaliation.

Both students received suspensions; the classmate for fighting, Wisemore for her Facebook post. "It was very colorful language I don't approve of, but I didn't like the fact the school stepped into my home," said Christy Wisemore, Megan's mother. "That's her constitutional right to write what she feels."

## The Protection of Student Speech

The First Amendment protection of student speech is grounded in the seminal case *Tinker v. Des Moines Independent Community School District* (1969). In *Tinker*, three public high school students were suspended for wearing black armbands to protest the Vietnam War. They successfully challenged the school's policy prohibiting the armbands, and in the process the Supreme Court created a new standard of review for student speech. Under this standard, school officials

Justin Silverman, "Keeping Online Speech Outside the Schoolhouse Gate," Citizen Media Law Project, March 17, 2010. www.citmedialaw.com. Reproduced by permission.

may prohibit or punish student speech only if the speech would "materially and substantially interfere with the requirements of appropriate discipline in the operation of the school."

The problem, however, is that social media provides students with a large platform from which off-campus speech can spill into the classroom. Though students have used services such as Facebook and MySpace for several years now, courts are still struggling to balance their First Amendment rights with the disruption their speech may cause on school grounds.

## Two Recent Cases

Consider two recent 3rd Circuit of Appeals cases. Both involved high school students who were suspended for creating fake MySpace profiles on which they insulted their principals. In *Layshock v. Hermitage School District* [2010], the court found that school officials should not have suspended a student who described his principal as, among other things, a "big whore" who smoked a "big blunt." In *J.S. v. Blue Mountain [School District* (2010)], the court upheld the suspension of a student who called her principal a "tight ass" who liked "hitting on students and their parents."

---

*As offensive as their comments may be, those students shouldn't be punished unless that speech enters the classroom and causes a disturbance.*

---

As the *Legal Intelligencer* explained: In *Layshock*, a unanimous three-judge panel declared that punishing students for off-campus speech violates their First Amendment rights. But the *Blue Mountain* panel split, voting 2-1 that students may be punished for lewd speech on the Internet about school officials that has the potential to create a substantial disturbance at school.

Forty-one years after *Tinker*, courts are waffling between interfering and *potentially* interfering. If there isn't consistency in cases such as these, students like Wisemore could be without recourse. Further, all other students with a Facebook account will risk suspension any time they update their status. As Justice [Abe] Fortas famously said in *Tinker*: Students do not shed their constitutional rights to freedom of speech at the schoolhouse gate. Yet at least some courts now seem willing to ask students to shed them before they even leave home.

It doesn't need to be that way. Courts should follow *Tinker* and expect schools to do so as well. Wisemore didn't interfere with her school when she posted to Facebook. Wisemore's classmate brought that speech into the classroom and caused a disturbance by starting a fight. That classmate should be the only student suspended. The comments made by the two 3rd Circuit plaintiffs didn't interfere with the schooling of any students. They targeted principals, and as offensive as their comments may be, those students shouldn't be punished unless that speech enters the classroom and causes a disturbance. For those who are the subject of online rants, there are legal remedies available when the speech is actionable, such as laws against libel and harassment.

## The Issue of Cyberbullying

What's complicating matters is the panic over cyberbullying. High-profile suicides, like those of Megan Meier and Phoebe Prince, can make the words of Wisemore seem more threatening. Cyberbullying is a problem because targeted students assume everyone is reading about them simply because the comments are online. But just because anyone can read the comments, doesn't mean everyone *is* actually reading those comments. The classmate that attacked Wisemore is claiming she was cyberbullied, despite the fact that Wisemore made her comment to a private group of friends. Still, school officials suspended Wisemore.

Many states are enacting cyberbullying laws to help combat hurtful and harassing online speech. Missouri enacted its own law two years ago in response to the suicide of Megan Meier, who lived in the state. Responding to the death of Prince, the Massachusetts Senate approved a bill last week [March 11, 2010] that would prohibit the use of e-mails, text messages, Internet postings and other electronic means to create a hostile school environment. This focus on creating "a hostile school environment" seems to be the right approach because the focus is within the schoolhouse gates, not beyond them. Drafters of that bill made clear that "nothing in this section shall be construed to abridge the rights of students that are protected by the First Amendment."

But that, unfortunately, is the problem. Those First Amendment rights have yet to be clearly defined.

# Random Student Drug Testing Is an Important Tool for Drug Prevention

*Student Drug-Testing Institute*

*The Student Drug-Testing Institute was established by the US Department of Education's Office of Safe and Drug-Free Schools to provide information on student drug testing programs.*

Random student drug testing is foremost a prevention program. Drug testing is one of several tools that schools can use as part of a comprehensive drug prevention effort. Administrators, faculty, and students at schools that conduct testing view random testing as a deterrent, and it gives students a reason to resist peer pressure to try or use drugs. Drug testing can identify students who have started using drugs so that interventions can occur early, or identify students who already have drug problems, so they can be referred for assessment, counseling, or treatment. Drug abuse not only interferes with a student's ability to learn, but it can also disrupt the teaching environment, affecting other students as well. Each school or school district that wants to start a program needs to involve the entire community in determining whether student drug testing is right for their specific situation.

## Student Drug Use

*How many students actually use drugs?*

Although drug use among America's youth has declined in recent years, many young people continue to abuse harmful substances. The 2008 Monitoring the Future survey shows that drug use among school-age youth has been in a state of decline since the 1990s; however, the proportions of 8th- and

Student Drug-Testing Institute, *Frequently Asked Questions About Student Drug Testing*, US Department of Education, June 2009. http://sdti.ed.gov.

12th-grade students indicating any use of an illicit drug in the 12 months prior to the survey showed rather modest increases since the previous year. Nearly half of 12th graders said that they have used drugs in their lifetime, and almost one-third said that they use marijuana at least monthly. According to another survey conducted in 2006, an estimated 20.4 million Americans aged 12 or older (8.3 percent of the population) were current illicit drug users, using within the past month.

Like use of other illicit drugs, steroid usage has seen a decline since usage peaked among male teens in 1999. However, steroid abuse is still a problem for many young people. The 2008 Monitoring the Future data show that 1.2 percent of 8th graders, 1.4 percent of 10th graders, and 2.5 percent of 12th graders reported using steroids at least once in their lifetime. A survey sponsored by the Centers for Disease Control and Prevention (CDC) reported that 3.9 percent of all high school students surveyed in 2007 reported use of steroid pills/shots without a doctor's prescription at some point in their lives. This figure includes 4.8 percent of 9th graders, 3.7 percent of 10th graders, 3.1 percent of 11th graders, and 3.8 percent of 12th graders.

---

*The expectation that they may be randomly tested is enough to make some students stop using drugs.*

---

Prescription drug abuse is also high and is increasing. The 2008 Monitoring the Future data indicate that 15.4 percent of 12th graders reported using a prescription drug nonmedically within the past year. Vicodin, an opiate pain reliever, continues to be abused at unacceptably high levels. Many of the drugs used by 12th graders are prescription drugs or, in the case of cough medicine, are available over the counter.

Despite some declines in drug use, much remains to be done. Youth still face a barrage of media messages and peer pressure that promotes drug use. Random student drug-testing programs are effective prevention strategies to help adolescents refuse drugs, when offered.

## Student Drug Testing

*How can schools determine if there is a need for a drug-testing program?*

Communities first need to identify their drug problems. This becomes the basis of developing a consensus for student drug testing. Schools must first determine whether there is a need for testing. Such a need can be determined from student drug-use surveys; reports by teachers and other school staff about student drug use; reports about drug use from parents and others in the community; and from discoveries of drugs, drug paraphernalia, or residues at school.

*Is student drug testing a stand-alone solution, or do schools need other programs to prevent and reduce drug use?*

Drug testing should never be undertaken as a stand-alone response to a drug problem. If testing is done, it should be one component of a comprehensive prevention and intervention program in compliance with local, state, and federal laws, with the common goal of reducing students' use of illegal drugs and misuse of prescription drugs.

*What are the benefits of drug testing?*

Drug use can turn into abuse and then into addiction, trapping users in a vicious cycle that can ruin lives and destroy families. Studies have shown drug testing to be an effective tool in preventing student drug use. The expectation that they may be randomly tested is enough to make some students stop using drugs—or never start in the first place. School-based drug testing is also an excellent tool for getting students who use drugs the help they need.

According to the 2007 National Survey on Drug Use and Health students who use drugs are statistically more likely to drop out of school, bring guns to school, steal, and be involved in fighting or other delinquent behavior. Drug abuse not only interferes with a student's ability to learn, it also disrupts the orderly environment necessary for all students to succeed. Obviously, reducing the likelihood of these disruptive behaviors benefits everyone involved in a school environment.

## The Dangers of Teen Drug Use

*Why are teens particularly vulnerable?*

Teens are especially vulnerable to drug abuse when the brain and body are still developing. Most teens do not use drugs, but for those that do, it can lead to a wide range of adverse effects on the brain, the body, behavior, and health.

*Short term*: Even a single use of an intoxicating drug can affect a person's judgment and decision making—resulting in accidents, poor performance in a school or sports activity, unplanned risky behavior, and the risk of overdosing.

*Long term*: Repeated drug abuse can lead to serious problems, such as poor academic outcomes, mood changes (depending on the drug: depression, anxiety, paranoia, psychosis), and social or family problems caused or worsened by drugs. Repeated drug use can also lead to the disease of addiction. Studies show that the earlier a teen begins using drugs, the more likely he or she will develop a substance abuse problem or addiction. Conversely, if teens stay away from drugs while in high school, they are less likely to develop a substance abuse problem later in life.

## The Research About Student Drug Testing

*What has research determined about the utility of random drug tests in schools?*

There is not very much research in this area and early research shows mixed results. A study published in 2007 found that student athletes who participated in randomized drug testing had overall rates of drug use similar to students who did not take part in the program, and in fact, some indicators of future drug abuse increased among those participating in the drug-testing program.

In another study, Hunterdon Central Regional High School in New Jersey saw significant reductions in 20 of 28 drug-use categories after 2 years of a drug-testing program (e.g., cocaine use by seniors dropped from 13 percent to 4 percent). A third study, from Ball State University, showed that 73 percent of high school principals reported a reduction in drug use among students subjected to a drug-testing policy, but only 2 percent reported an increase. Because of the limited number of studies on this topic, more research is warranted.

*Are there any current randomized control studies about the impact of mandatory random student drug testing on the reduction of student substance use?*

Yes, RMC Research is conducting a national impact evaluation of mandatory random student drug testing. The four-year study is funded by the U.S. Department of Education's Institute of Education Sciences to assess the effects of school-based mandatory random drug-testing programs. The study population comprises school districts and schools that received grants from the Office of Safe and Drug-Free Schools to implement mandatory random student drug testing. The study includes the collection of school-level drug testing results and data garnered through student surveys, school-wide record review, and staff interviews. The study, designed as a cluster randomized control trial, is the first of its sort to examine this topic and will contribute to knowledge about the impact of mandatory random student drug testing on the reduction of student substance use. Preliminary results are expected in November 2009. [There are no results yet as of July 2010.]

## Student Drug Testing and Legal Matters

*Does the federal government mandate student drug testing?*

No. The federal government recognizes drug testing as one tool that local schools can choose as a component of a broad drug prevention effort. Each school or school district that wants to start a program needs to involve the entire community in determining whether student drug testing is right for their specific situation.

*What have the courts said?*

The Supreme Court of the United States first determined that drug testing of student athletes is constitutional in a June 1995 decision. Voting 6 to 3 in *Vernonia School District v. Acton* the court upheld the constitutionality of a policy requiring student athletes to submit to random drug testing.

In June 2002, the U.S. Supreme Court broadened the authority of public schools to test students for illegal drugs. Voting 5 to 4 in *Board of Education v. Earls*, the court ruled to allow random drug tests for all middle and high school students participating in competitive extracurricular activities. The ruling greatly expanded the scope of school drug testing.

*Just because the U.S Supreme Court ruled that student drug testing for adolescents in competitive extracurricular activities is constitutional, does that mean it is legal in my city or state?*

A school or school district interested in adopting a student drug-testing program should seek legal expertise so that it complies with all federal, state, and local laws. Individual state constitutions and court rulings may dictate different legal thresholds for allowing student drug testing. Communities interested in starting a student drug-testing program should become familiar with the law in their respective states to ensure proper compliance....

## The Consequences of a Positive Drug Test

*What are the consequences if a student tests positive for drugs in a random drug test?*

The primary purpose of random drug testing is not to punish students who use drugs but to prevent drug dependence and to help drug-dependent students become drug free. Students testing positive may require intervention before they become dependent on drugs. Interventions can include follow-up testing, assessment, counseling, and a referral to a drug treatment program to begin the recovery process. However, a student should not face any academically or legally punitive consequences because of a confirmed positive random test.

---

*The U.S. Supreme Court has ruled that student drug testing is permissible, but must be done confidentially.*

---

*If a student tests positive for drugs, are schools responsible for paying for drug treatment?*

No; however, well-crafted drug-testing programs will include qualified health and drug treatment professionals to aid in assessing students who test positive. Some parents may be unable to accept their child's use or not know how to help their child. It is important that schools have resources available to help educate parents on the problem and help them choose how to intervene or how to get their child needed professional treatment.

## Student Privacy Rights

*Is drug testing a violation of students' privacy rights?*

This concern usually stems from a misunderstanding of the purpose of student drug testing. Foremost, the U.S. Supreme Court has ruled that student drug testing is permissible, but must be done confidentially. Schools have a responsibility to respect students' privacy, so it is vital that only the people who need to know the test results see them—parents, the student, and a school administrator, for example. The results should not be shared with anyone else, not even teachers. The purpose is not to expose and punish children for drug use, but to deter use, intervene early with those who have just begun to use, and to provide help to those who have become dependent.

Student drug-testing records should also be kept strictly confidential in accordance with the Family Educational Rights and Privacy Act (FERPA), a federal law that protects the privacy of student education records. The law applies to all schools that receive funds under an applicable program of the U.S. Department of Education. Student drug-testing activities are often also covered under the Protection of Pupil Rights Amendment (PPRA). . . .

## The Student Drug-Testing Process

*What testing methods are available?*

There are several testing methods available for different types of specimens, including urine, hair, oral fluids, and sweat (patch). These methods vary in cost, reliability, drugs detected, and detection period. Schools should determine their needs and choose the method that best suits their requirements, as long as the testing procedures are conducted by a reliable source, such as a certified or nationally accredited drug-testing company or a hospital.

*For which drugs can and should students be tested?*

Various testing methods normally test for a "panel" of drugs. Typically, a drug panel tests for marijuana, cocaine, opioids, amphetamines, and PCP [phencyclidine]. If a school or community has a particular problem with other drugs, such as tobacco, ecstasy (MDMA), gamma-hydroxybutyrate (GHB), or steroids, they can include testing for these drugs.

*How accurate are drug tests? Is there a possibility a test could give a false positive?*

Screening tests are very accurate but not 100 percent accurate. Usually samples are divided so if an initial test is positive, a confirmation test can be conducted.

## The Detection of Drugs

*Can students "beat" the tests?*

Many drug-using students are aware of techniques that supposedly detoxify their systems or mask their drug use. Popular magazines and Internet sites give advice on how to dilute urine samples, and there are even companies that sell drug-free "clean" urine or products designed to distort test results. A number of techniques and products are focused on urine tests for marijuana, but masking products increasingly are becoming available for tests of hair, oral fluids, and multiple drugs.

Most of these products do not work, are very costly, can be identified in the testing process, and must be readily available at the random time of testing. Moreover, even if the specific drug is successfully masked, the masking product itself can be detected, in which case the student using it would become an obvious candidate for additional screening and attention. In fact, some testing programs consider a test "positive" if a masking product is detected.

*What about alcohol?*

Alcohol is a drug and a serious problem among young people. However, alcohol does not remain in the blood long enough for most tests to detect recent use. Breathalyzers and oral fluid tests can detect current use, and can be used to measure impairment. The ethyl glucuronide (EtG) test can be used to detect recent alcohol use; however, the National Institute on Drug Abuse has questioned the reliability of this test. Adolescents with substance abuse problems are often polydrug users (they use more than one drug), so identifying a problem with an illicit or prescription drug may suggest an alcohol problem.

# Schools Need Broad Authority to Conduct Searches of Students

*National School Boards Association and American Association of School Administrators*

*The National School Boards Association is an organization representing state associations of school boards, and the American Association of School Administrators is a professional organization for educational leaders.*

In [*New Jersey v.*] *T.L.O.* [(1985)], this Court [US Supreme Court] appropriately recognized that school officials responsible for maintaining safe and orderly learning environments need more flexibility than the probable cause standard under the Fourth Amendment generally permits. To provide this flexibility, the Court adopted a reasonable suspicion standard that accords deference to the judgments of school personnel in making risk assessments regarding the students suspected of violating school rules or the law. While this ruling thus eased the constitutional burdens on school leaders, the practical application of *T.L.O.* has led to confusion among both judges and educators.

## The *T.L.O.* Test for Student Searches

The first prong of the *T.L.O.* test requires courts to assess whether the search was justified at its inception. The lower courts' inconsistent application of this prong has resulted in the sending of mixed messages to educators as to how they must evaluate information about alleged student misconduct that raises health and safety concerns and determine an appropriate course of action. Here [in the case of *Safford Unified*

National School Boards Association and American Association of School Administrators, amici curiae brief in support of petitioners in *Safford Unified School Dist. #1 v. April Redding*, March 4, 2009. Reproduced by permission.

*School District #1 v. April Redding*], the assistant principal received relevant information from both students and adults and knew of past incidents of student drug abuse that caused serious bodily harm. However, in the Ninth Circuit's estimation [finding the student search to be unconstitutional], the assistant principal did not have sufficient basis for conducting a search of the student's clothes to find the drugs students were reportedly planning to ingest hours later.

---

*In T.L.O., this Court appropriately recognized that school officials . . . need more flexibility than the probable cause standard under the Fourth Amendment generally permits.*

---

Another area of confusion arises from the justified-at-inception prong of the *T.L.O.* test as applied to searches with varying levels of privacy intrusion. Here, for example, the educators were looking for prescription pills—obviously a small item that could easily be concealed. Only after the initial minimally intrusive attempts turned up nothing did the search progress. Pursuant to the Ninth Circuit's decision, both educators and courts must continuously reassess the propriety of the search, using the justified-at-inception analysis, whenever the level of intrusion escalates during the search. Nothing in *T.L.O.* mandates a new level of inquiry under the justified-at-inception prong as the search progresses unless new evidence is found along the way.

The second part of the *T.L.O.* test, reasonable-in-scope, also has led to confusing and divergent guidance. When the objective of the search is to determine whether the student has concealed small items, especially items with potential for harm, then the search may need to be more intrusive to detect the items. The lower courts have recognized this practicality. The Ninth Circuit's opinion, however, rejects this recognition, broadly calling into question the ability of school officials to make all practical searches—both minimally intrusive and more intrusive. Without clarification of the reasonable-in-scope prong, educators will be hindered in their ability to enforce rules that prohibit possession of potentially dangerous, small items such as drugs.

---

*If an educator has reasonable suspicion that a student is involved in misconduct . . . she should not have to reconsider whether the degree of suspicion justifies each level of privacy intrusion.*

---

The *T.L.O.* decision included analyzing the "nature of the infraction" as part of its framework for determining the constitutionality of school searches, but the *T.L.O.* Court explicitly declined to preclude certain infractions that some might regard as too "trivial." The federal courts have provided scant guidance to educators regarding the application of the "nature of the infraction" factor. The Ninth Circuit's application of this factor seems directly at odds with what the *T.L.O.* Court had in mind. Despite this Court's admonition to avoid second-guessing educators about the importance of particular school rules, the Ninth Circuit simply dismissed the importance of the educator's concerns for student safety here. That attitude colored the entire decision. . . .

## The Level of Suspicion Needed

The most disconcerting part of the Ninth Circuit's analysis of the justified-at-inception prong is its creation of a "sliding scale" requirement as to suspicion. The Ninth Circuit suggests that, as the intrusiveness of a search increases, educators will need a higher level of suspicion to conduct the search. This is in direct conflict with *T.L.O.*'s holding that educators need only reasonable suspicion—nothing more—to conduct a student search. To the extent that the Ninth Circuit now requires a level of suspicion higher than reasonable suspicion for some student searches to be justified at their inception, this Court should reaffirm the reasonable suspicion standard enunciated in *T.L.O.* and negate any suggestion that a sliding scale is to be used in the justified-at-inception inquiry. To emphasize Petitioners' argument, the issue that needs to be addressed in the first prong is not whether a *strip* search is justified at its inception, but whether a search is justified at its inception.

This case provides the opportunity for this Court to clear up the confusion because, unlike in *T.L.O.*, the educator in this case did not conduct two separate searches. In *T.L.O.*, two separate justified-at-inception inquiries were necessary because there were two separate searches looking for evidence of two different types of misconduct. Here, the assistant principal was only looking for evidence relating to the possession and distribution of prescription drugs. In cases such as this involving only one suspected type of misconduct, *Amici* [the authors of the brief] submit that only one justified-at-inception inquiry is required. If an educator has reasonable suspicion that a student is involved in misconduct, then as long as she is looking for evidence of the original misconduct, she should not have to reconsider whether the degree of suspicion justifies each level of privacy intrusion. The proper analysis for determining the reasonableness of a progressive search under *T.L.O.* is the reasonable-in-scope prong.

## The Problem with a Sliding Scale

By adopting a standard that increases the level of suspicion required of educators to perform more invasive searches, the Ninth Circuit has blurred the line between the justified-at-inception and the reasonable-in-scope prongs. These two prongs, as *T.L.O.* held, are separate and distinct. If an educator has reasonable suspicion to search a student, she is justified at the inception of the search. If there is no reasonable suspicion, the search should not occur. However, once the educator has reasonable suspicion, she need not reassess the level of suspicion when deciding whether the scope of the search is reasonable. As the Court held in *T.L.O.*, a search justified at its inception is reasonable in scope "when the measures adopted are reasonably related to the objectives of the search and not excessively intrusive in light of the age and sex of the student and the nature of the infraction." The level of suspicion is completely irrelevant to whether a search satisfies the reasonable-in-scope prong. As discussed below, provided the search is designed to find the objects sought and is not excessively intrusive based on the factors of age, sex, and the nature of the infraction, the search should be deemed reasonable in scope, with no reversion to the justified-at-inception prong and no repeat inquiry into the level of suspicion. Any other analysis is contrary to *T.L.O.*

Consider the confusion that the Ninth Circuit's sliding scale would have on other student searches. For example, what would be the proper justified-at-inception standard for a search of a female student where the objective of the search is to turn up evidence that she is selling ecstasy pills to other students? The student has a car, locker, desk, book bag, athletic bag, and a purse. Within the purse are numerous open and zippered pockets. Within the zippered pockets are wallets and smaller zippered bags. Within the book bag is a written journal, digital music player, cell phone, and digital camera. Within the athletic bag is a toiletries bag. The student herself is wearing three layers of clothing, a hat, socks, and shoes. Imagine how complicated it would be for an educator to follow the Ninth Circuit's progressive search analysis for each level of intrusion by considering each item examined to constitute a separate search and recalculating not only the reasonable scope of the search relative to its objectives and its intrusiveness in light of the student's age and sex and the nature of the infraction, but also the initial degree of suspicion. That is not and should not be the standard educators must follow. . . .

## Guidelines for Educators

This Court can clarify the constitutional expectation of educators under *T.L.O.*'s reasonable-in-scope prong without inadvertently exposing students to more danger, needlessly complicating the law, or undermining the sensible judicial deference to educators.

First, under the objectives-of-the-search part of the reasonable-in-scope prong it would be reasonable for the Court to emphasize the need for educators, as occurred in this case, first to attempt to search less intrusively for the objective of the search. Although the exigencies of some extreme situations may not always permit the exhaustion of all less intrusive means of searching, educators should attempt to tailor their searches to start with less intrusive methods before escalating, where appropriate, to more intrusive methods.

---

*The higher the potential danger of the alleged student misconduct, the more deference courts should give educators regarding the scope of the search.*

---

Similarly, the age and gender factors as to intrusiveness were not explained in *T.L.O.* but could be here. For the gender factor, it would be presumptively unreasonable for an educator of one gender to perform an invasive search of a student of the opposite gender, particular one involving removal of other than outer clothing like coats and hats. As for the age factor, it is reasonable to require educators to restrict themselves to less invasive searches for younger students. With the age factor, there may also be the added consideration of the student's experience with privacy intrusions.

## The Need for Deference to Educators

*Amici*'s primary concern regarding the Ninth Circuit's application of *T.L.O.* concerns the nature-of-the-infraction factor of intrusiveness. Although the type of student misconduct at issue should be irrelevant to the justified-at-inception inquiry, it is the focus of the nature-of-the-infraction factor. Generally speaking, the higher the potential danger of the alleged student misconduct, the more deference courts should give educators regarding the scope of the search.

*Amici* do not suggest that educators are free from judicial oversight. Public schools are governmental entities, public school educators must comply with the Constitution, and a student search can be too intrusive for the Fourth Amendment to tolerate.

Here, however, the Ninth Circuit neglected to accord school officials the flexibility and deference this Court has deemed appropriate to address effectively the serious problem of student drug abuse. Instead, the Ninth Circuit unwisely substituted its own judgment that the threat of several students ingesting prescription strength drugs did not pose the necessary degree of harm to student health and welfare that would justify searching the student's person and clothing. This is in direct conflict with this Court's precedent.

## The Need to Combat Drug Abuse

*T.L.O.* itself represents this Court's first recognition of the need to defer to school officials' efforts to combat drug abuse. "Maintaining order in the classroom has never been easy," the Court noted, "but in recent years, school disorder has often taken particularly ugly forms: drug use and violent crime in the schools have become major social problems." Because of this alarming trend, the Court appropriately acknowledged "that maintaining security and order in the schools requires a certain degree of flexibility in school disciplinary procedures, and we have respected the value of preserving the informality of the student-teacher relationship."

The Court continued this deferential approach in analyzing the constitutionality of the student drug testing policies at issue in [*Vernonia School District v.*] *Acton* [(1995)] and [*Board of Education v.*] *Earls* [(2002)]. In *Acton*, this Court emphasized society's interest in combating student drug use. "That the nature of the concern is important—indeed, perhaps compelling—can hardly be doubted. Deterring drug use by our nation's schoolchildren is at least as important as enhancing efficient enforcement of the nation's laws against the importation of drugs." The Court explained that "[s]chool years are the time when the physical, psychological, and addictive effects of drugs are most severe." Discussing further the systemic problem of drug abuse as a rationale for deferring to educators' judgment about how to combat the problem, the Court wrote that "of course the effects of a drug-infested school are visited not just upon the users, but upon the entire student body and faculty, as the educational process is disrupted." In *Earls*, the Court reiterated its view that deference to educators when combating drug abuse is appropriate in deciding the constitutionality of school searches. "The drug abuse problem among our nation's youth has hardly abated since [*Acton*] was decided in 1995. In fact evidence suggests that it has only grown worse." Nor has the concern abated since *Earls* was decided. In some ways, at least, it has grown worse. For example, the most recent data on female juvenile arrests reveals that drug-related arrests have increased by 15 percent since 1997.

The Court most recently reaffirmed the need for deference in *Morse* [*v. Frederick* (2007)]. While *Morse* did not address a student search, the Court again noted the critical importance of combating student drug use by stating "that schools may take steps to safeguard those entrusted to their care from speech that can reasonably be regarded as encouraging illegal drug use." It would be a strange result indeed if the law allows educators to protect students from speech promoting drug use but unduly constrains them from actually attempting to find and confiscate the drugs themselves when there are reasonable grounds to believe drugs are present at school.

By failing to defer to educators when it substituted its own ideas of which drug threats are important and which are not, the Ninth Circuit has created the very atmosphere of turning the "judge's chambers into the principal's office" against which Justice [Stephen] Breyer warned in his concurring opinion in *Morse*:

> Students will test the limits of acceptable behavior in myriad ways better known to schoolteachers than to judges; school officials need a degree of flexible authority to respond to disciplinary challenges; and the law has always considered the relationship between teachers and students special. Under these circumstances, the more detailed the Court's supervision becomes, the more likely its law will engender further disputes among teachers and students. Consequently, larger numbers of those disputes will likely make their way from the schoolhouse to the courthouse. Yet no one wishes to substitute courts for school boards, or to turn the judge's chambers into the principal's office.

## The Dangers of Prescription and OTC Drugs

Now more than ever, schools are in the forefront of addressing dangers to our youth, including their growing abuse of prescription drugs. The Office of National Drug Control Policy (ONDCP) found in 2006 that, "more than 2.1 million teens abused prescription drugs." Indeed, the report states that "more young people ages 12–17 abuse prescription drugs than any illicit drug except marijuana—more than cocaine, heroin, and methamphetamine combined." Even more alarming, 12- to 13-year-olds indicate that prescription drugs are their drug of choice. In a more recent report, the ONDCP stated that "2.5 million people aged 12 or older used prescription drugs nonmedically for the first time. This means there are approximately 7,000 new prescription drugs abusers every day." [According to a 2008 Monitoring the Future survey,] most prescription drugs have "showed steady growth in use outside of their legitimate medical use through most of the 1990s. . . . As a result, they have become a relatively more important part of the nation's drug abuse problem."

The ONDCP also identified teenaged girls as having a heightened risk for prescription drug abuse. ONDCP reported "that females are at particular risk for prescription drug abuse, with higher rates of abuse among teen girls, more emergency room visits among young women, and higher rates of treatment admissions for dependence on some prescription drugs among females."

Further, and contrary to the Ninth Circuit's dismissal of any imminent danger, the ONDCP report states that "[t]here has been a dramatic increase in the number of poisonings and even deaths associated with the abuse of prescription and OTC [over-the-counter] drugs." The National Institute on Drug Abuse (NIDA) reports that abuse of prescription or OTC drugs can have a number of adverse physical and psychological effects, including impairing motor function, life-threatening respiratory and heart problems, hostility, paranoia, and depression. Unfortunately, prescription painkillers have been implicated in nearly 40 percent of the 22,400 annual drug overdose deaths most recently recorded. This number is compared to the 17,000 deaths attributed to homicide in the same year.

## The Importance of School Intervention

Because the Ninth Circuit did not view prescription strength versions of OTC drugs as an imminent threat, it discounted the educator's concern in this case. Not only is it unwise to exclude certain prescription drugs from discussion of prescription drug abuse, but even OTC drugs are being abused more and more. OTC drug abuse is of particular concern "given the easy access teens have to these products."

One major reason why schools are a natural battleground for the war against prescription and OTC drug abuse is the source of these drugs. More than half of surveyed high school seniors [by Monitoring the Future] reported their source of prescription drugs "was getting them free from a friend or relative, followed 'closely by being sold the drugs by a friend or relative. . . . Only about a fifth to a quarter of users of these drugs said that they had bought them from a dealer or stranger. Clearly the informal networks of relatives and friends play a major role in the distribution of these prescription drugs to young users."

---

*It is prudent to follow precedent and consider recent studies by giving educators relatively more deference when the student misconduct at issue involves drugs.*

---

Responsible school administrators are well aware of the national trends in student drug abuse and are in a unique position to understand the substance abuse patterns in their own schools and communities, to take these problems seriously, and to use appropriate measures to respond on an educational as well as disciplinary level. But the message the Ninth Circuit's ruling sends is that prescription and OTC drug abuse is not significant enough a problem to warrant immediate intervention by school personnel who have reason to believe that students are planning to ingest drugs neither prescribed by a health care professional nor provided by their parents. While public health authorities are calling loudly for increased awareness of this issue, the Ninth Circuit dismissed the concern as trifling, if not pretextual. The Ninth Circuit's refusal to accord appropriate deference to school officials makes the difficult job of protecting student health and welfare even harder.

## Giving Educators Room to Search

This Court should provide more detailed guidance regarding the nature-of-the-infraction factor under the reasonable-in-scope prong. In doing so, it is prudent to follow precedent and consider recent studies by giving educators relatively more deference when the student misconduct at issue involves drugs.

*Amici* offer some suggestions for this Court as it further defines and interprets the nature-of-the-infraction factor. First and most important, this Court should clarify that the more a suspected student's conduct poses a potential safety risk on campus or at a school-sponsored event, the more deference should be given to educators in making decisions about the appropriate scope of a search. Deference need not be abject, but this case demonstrates the problems that arise when a court strays too far from the deferential approach. That said, where the suspected student misconduct poses no potential safety concern, the Court may wish to indicate that a highly invasive search is presumptively unreasonable.

In addition, there should be no doubt that the unapproved use or distribution at school of drugs—whether illicit, prescription, or OTC—falls into the category of misconduct involving potential harm. The determination of whether a student's conduct poses a safety hazard should not incorporate the benefit of hindsight. Nor should an educator be forced to research the harmful effects of certain substances before making a decision to conduct a search. While educators are especially well attuned to trends like drug abuse, they are neither pharmacists nor law enforcement officials and should not be expected to know precisely how certain drugs affect students, either alone or in combination with other substances.

# Schools Can Rightfully Interfere with Student Speech off Campus

*John Roberts*

*John Roberts is chief justice of the US Supreme Court. He was appointed by President George W. Bush in 2005.*

At a school-sanctioned and school-supervised event, a high school principal saw some of her students unfurl a large banner conveying a message she reasonably regarded as promoting illegal drug use. Consistent with established school policy prohibiting such messages at school events, the principal directed the students to take down the banner. One student—among those who had brought the banner to the event—refused to do so. The principal confiscated the banner and later suspended the student. The Ninth Circuit held that the principal's actions violated the First Amendment, and that the student could sue the principal for damages.

Our cases make clear that students do not "shed their constitutional rights to freedom of speech or expression at the schoolhouse gate" [*Tinker v. Des Moines Independent Community School District* (1969)]. At the same time, we have held that "the constitutional rights of students in public school are not automatically coextensive with the rights of adults in other settings" [*Bethel School District No. 403 v. Fraser* (1986)], and that the rights of students "must be 'applied in light of the special characteristics of the school environment'" [*Hazelwood School District v. Kuhlmeier* (1988) (quoting *Tinker*)]. Consistent with these principles, we hold that schools may take steps to safeguard those entrusted to their care from speech that can reasonably be regarded as encouraging illegal drug use. We conclude that the school officials in this case did

John Roberts, *Morse v. Frederick*, June 25, 2007.

not violate the First Amendment by confiscating the pro-drug banner and suspending the student responsible for it.

## A School Suspension for Speech

On January 24, 2002, the Olympic Torch Relay passed through Juneau, Alaska, on its way to the winter games in Salt Lake City, Utah. The torchbearers were to proceed along a street in front of Juneau-Douglas High School (JDHS) while school was in session. Petitioner Deborah Morse, the school principal, decided to permit staff and students to participate in the Torch Relay as an approved social event or class trip. Students were allowed to leave class to observe the relay from either side of the street. Teachers and administrative officials monitored the students' actions.

Respondent Joseph Frederick, a JDHS senior, was late to school that day. When he arrived, he joined his friends (all but one of whom were JDHS students) across the street from the school to watch the event. Not all the students waited patiently. Some became rambunctious, throwing plastic cola bottles and snowballs and scuffling with their classmates. As the torchbearers and camera crews passed by, Frederick and his friends unfurled a 14-foot banner bearing the phrase: "BONG HiTS 4 JESUS." The large banner was easily readable by the students on the other side of the street.

Principal Morse immediately crossed the street and demanded that the banner be taken down. Everyone but Frederick complied. Morse confiscated the banner and told Frederick to report to her office, where she suspended him for 10 days. Morse later explained that she told Frederick to take the banner down because she thought it encouraged illegal drug use, in violation of established school policy. Juneau School Board Policy No. 5520 states: "The Board specifically prohibits any assembly or public expression that . . . advocates the use of substances that are illegal to minors. . . ." In addition, Juneau School Board Policy No. 5850 subjects "[p]upils who participate in approved social events and class trips" to the same student conduct rules that apply during the regular school program.

## The Superintendent's Reasoning

Frederick administratively appealed his suspension, but the Juneau School District Superintendent upheld it, limiting it to time served (8 days). In a memorandum setting forth his reasons, the superintendent determined that Frederick had displayed his banner "in the midst of his fellow students, during school hours, at a school-sanctioned activity." He further explained that Frederick "was not disciplined because the principal of the school 'disagreed' with his message, but because his speech appeared to advocate the use of illegal drugs."

The superintendent continued:

"The commonsense understanding of the phrase 'bong hits' is that it is a reference to a means of smoking marijuana. Given [Frederick's] inability or unwillingness to express any other credible meaning for the phrase, I can only agree with the principal and countless others who saw the banner as advocating the use of illegal drugs. [Frederick's] speech was not political. He was not advocating the legalization of marijuana or promoting a religious belief. He was displaying a fairly silly message promoting illegal drug usage in the midst of a school activity, for the benefit of television cameras covering the Torch Relay. [Frederick's] speech was potentially disruptive to the event and clearly disruptive of and inconsistent with the school's educational mission to educate students about the dangers of illegal drugs and to discourage their use."

Relying on our decision in *Fraser*, the superintendent concluded that the principal's actions were permissible because Frederick's banner was "speech or action that intrudes upon the work of the schools." The Juneau School District Board of Education upheld the suspension.

## The Lower Court Rulings

Frederick then filed suit under 42 U. S. C. §1983, alleging that the school board and Morse had violated his First Amendment rights. He sought declaratory and injunctive relief, unspecified compensatory damages, punitive damages, and attorney's fees. The District Court granted summary judgment for the school board and Morse, ruling that they were entitled to qualified immunity and that they had not infringed Frederick's First Amendment rights. The court found that Morse reasonably interpreted the banner as promoting illegal drug use—a message that "directly contravened the Board's policies relating to drug abuse prevention." Under the circumstances, the court held that "Morse had the authority, if not the obligation, to stop such messages at a school-sanctioned activity."

The Ninth Circuit reversed. Deciding that Frederick acted during a "school-authorized activit[y]," and "proceed[ing] on the basis that the banner expressed a positive sentiment about marijuana use," the court nonetheless found a violation of Frederick's First Amendment rights because the school punished Frederick without demonstrating that his speech gave rise to a "risk of substantial disruption." The court further concluded that Frederick's right to display his banner was so "clearly established" that a reasonable principal in Morse's position would have understood that her actions were unconstitutional, and that Morse was therefore not entitled to qualified immunity.

## A School Speech Issue

We granted certiorari [review of the case] on two questions: whether Frederick had a First Amendment right to wield his banner, and, if so, whether that right was so clearly established that the principal may be held liable for damages. We resolve the first question against Frederick, and therefore have no occasion to reach the second.

At the outset, we reject Frederick's argument that this is not a school speech case—as has every other authority to address the question. The event occurred during normal school hours. It was sanctioned by Principal Morse "as an approved social event or class trip," and the school district's rules expressly provide that pupils in "approved social events and class trips are subject to district rules for student conduct." Teachers and administrators were interspersed among the students and charged with supervising them. The high school band and cheerleaders performed. Frederick, standing among other JDHS students across the street from the school, directed his banner toward the school, making it plainly visible to most students. Under these circumstances, we agree with the superintendent that Frederick cannot "stand in the midst of his fellow students, during school hours, at a school-sanctioned activity and claim he is not at school." There is some uncertainty at the outer boundaries as to when courts should apply school speech precedents, but not on these facts.

---

*Principal Morse thought the banner would be interpreted by those viewing it as promoting illegal drug use, and that interpretation is plainly a reasonable one.*

---

## The Message of the Banner

The message on Frederick's banner is cryptic. It is no doubt offensive to some, perhaps amusing to others. To still others, it probably means nothing at all. Frederick himself claimed "that the words were just nonsense meant to attract television cameras." But Principal Morse thought the banner would be interpreted by those viewing it as promoting illegal drug use, and that interpretation is plainly a reasonable one.

As Morse later explained in a declaration, when she saw the sign, she thought that "the reference to a 'bong hit' would be widely understood by high school students and others as referring to smoking marijuana." She further believed that "display of the banner would be construed by students, District personnel, parents and others witnessing the display of the banner, as advocating or promoting illegal drug use"—in violation of school policy.

We agree with Morse. At least two interpretations of the words on the banner demonstrate that the sign advocated the use of illegal drugs. First, the phrase could be interpreted as an imperative: "[Take] bong hits . . ."—a message equivalent, as Morse explained in her declaration, to "smoke marijuana" or "use an illegal drug." Alternatively, the phrase could be viewed as celebrating drug use—"bong hits [are a good thing]," or "[we take] bong hits"—and we discern no meaningful distinction between celebrating illegal drug use in the midst of fellow students and outright advocacy or promotion.

## Alternative to the Pro-Drug Interpretation

The pro-drug interpretation of the banner gains further plausibility given the paucity of alternative meanings the banner might bear. The best Frederick can come up with is that the banner is "meaningless and funny." The dissent similarly refers to the sign's message as "curious," "ambiguous," "nonsense," "ridiculous," "obscure," "silly," "quixotic," and "stupid." Gibberish is surely a possible interpretation of the words on the banner, but it is not the only one, and dismissing the banner as meaningless ignores its undeniable reference to illegal drugs.

The dissent mentions Frederick's "credible and uncontradicted explanation for the message—he just wanted to get on television." But that is a description of Frederick's *motive* for displaying the banner; it is not an interpretation of what the banner says. The *way* Frederick was going to fulfill his ambition of appearing on television was by unfurling a pro-drug banner at a school event, in the presence of teachers and fellow students.

Elsewhere in its opinion, the dissent emphasizes the importance of political speech and the need to foster "national debate about a serious issue," as if to suggest that the banner is political speech. But not even Frederick argues that the banner conveys any sort of political or religious message. Contrary to the dissent's suggestion, this is plainly not a case about political debate over the criminalization of drug use or possession.

## The Restriction of Student Speech

The question thus becomes whether a principal may, consistent with the First Amendment, restrict student speech at a school event, when that speech is reasonably viewed as promoting illegal drug use. We hold that she may.

In *Tinker*, this Court made clear that "First Amendment rights, applied in light of the special characteristics of the school environment, are available to teachers and students." *Tinker* involved a group of high school students who decided to wear black armbands to protest the Vietnam War. School officials learned of the plan and then adopted a policy prohibiting students from wearing armbands. When several students nonetheless wore armbands to school, they were suspended. The students sued, claiming that their First Amendment rights had been violated, and this Court agreed.

---

*School boards have the authority to determine "what manner of speech in the classroom or in school assembly is inappropriate."*

---

*Tinker* held that student expression may not be suppressed unless school officials reasonably conclude that it will "materially and substantially disrupt the work and discipline of the school." The essential facts of *Tinker* are quite stark, implicating concerns at the heart of the First Amendment. The students sought to engage in political speech, using the armbands to express their "disapproval of the Vietnam hostilities and their advocacy of a truce, to make their views known, and, by their example, to influence others to adopt them." Political speech, of course, is "at the core of what the First Amendment is designed to protect" [*Virginia v. Black* (2003)]. The only interest the Court discerned underlying the school's actions was the "mere desire to avoid the discomfort and unpleasantness that always accompany an unpopular viewpoint," or "an urgent wish to avoid the controversy which might result from the expression" [*Tinker*]. That interest was not enough to justify banning "a silent, passive expression of opinion, unaccompanied by any disorder or disturbance."

## First Amendment Rights at School

This Court's next student speech case was *Fraser*. Matthew Fraser was suspended for delivering a speech before a high school assembly in which he employed what this Court called "an elaborate, graphic, and explicit sexual metaphor." Analyzing the case under *Tinker*, the District Court and Court of Appeals found no disruption, and therefore no basis for disciplining Fraser. This Court reversed, holding that the "School District acted entirely within its permissible authority in imposing sanctions upon Fraser in response to his offensively lewd and indecent speech."

The mode of analysis employed in *Fraser* is not entirely clear. The Court was plainly attuned to the content of Fraser's speech, citing the "marked distinction between the political 'message' of the armbands in *Tinker* and the sexual content of [Fraser's] speech." But the Court also reasoned that school boards have the authority to determine "what manner of speech in the classroom or in school assembly is inappropriate."

We need not resolve this debate to decide this case. For present purposes, it is enough to distill from *Fraser* two basic principles. First, *Fraser's* holding demonstrates that "the constitutional rights of students in public school are not automatically coextensive with the rights of adults in other settings." Had Fraser delivered the same speech in a public forum outside the school context, it would have been protected. In school, however, Fraser's First Amendment rights were circumscribed "in light of the special characteristics of the school environment" [*Tinker*]. Second, *Fraser* established that the mode of analysis set forth in *Tinker* is not absolute. Whatever approach *Fraser* employed, it certainly did not conduct the "substantial disruption" analysis prescribed by *Tinker*.

## More Latitude for School Authorities

Our most recent student speech case, *Kuhlmeier*, concerned "expressive activities that students, parents, and members of the public might reasonably perceive to bear the imprimatur of the school." Staff members of a high school newspaper sued their school when it chose not to publish two of their articles. The Court of Appeals analyzed the case under *Tinker*, ruling in favor of the students because it found no evidence of material disruption to class work or school discipline. This Court reversed, holding that "educators do not offend the First Amendment by exercising editorial control over the style and content of student speech in school-sponsored expressive activities so long as their actions are reasonably related to legitimate pedagogical concerns."

*Kuhlmeier* does not control this case because no one would reasonably believe that Frederick's banner bore the school's imprimatur. The case is nevertheless instructive because it confirms both principles cited above. *Kuhlmeier* acknowledged that schools may regulate some speech "even though the government could not censor similar speech outside the school." And, like *Fraser*, it confirms that the rule of *Tinker* is not the only basis for restricting student speech.

Drawing on the principles applied in our student speech cases, we have held in the Fourth Amendment context that "while children assuredly do not 'shed their constitutional rights ... at the schoolhouse gate,' ... the nature of those rights is what is appropriate for children in school" [*Vernonia School District v. Acton* (1995) (quoting *Tinker*)]. In particular, "the school setting requires some easing of the restrictions to which searches by public authorities are ordinarily subject" [*New Jersey v. T.L.O.* (1985)].

## A Compelling School Interest

Even more to the point, these cases also recognize that deterring drug use by schoolchildren is an "important—indeed, perhaps compelling" interest [*Vernonia*]. Drug abuse can cause severe and permanent damage to the health and well-being of young people:

> "School years are the time when the physical, psychological, and addictive effects of drugs are most severe. Maturing nervous systems are more critically impaired by intoxicants than mature ones are; childhood losses in learning are lifelong and profound; children grow chemically dependent more quickly than adults, and their record of recovery is depressingly poor. And of course the effects of a drug-infested school are visited not just upon the users, but upon the entire student body and faculty, as the educational process is disrupted."

Just five years ago, we wrote: "The drug abuse problem among our nation's youth has hardly abated since *Vernonia* was decided in 1995. In fact, evidence suggests that it has only grown worse" [*Earls*].

The problem remains serious today. About half of American 12th graders have used an illicit drug, as have more than a third of 10th graders and about one-fifth of 8th graders. Nearly one in four 12th graders has used an illicit drug in the past month. Some 25% of high schoolers say that they have been offered, sold, or given an illegal drug on school property within the past year.

Congress has declared that part of a school's job is educating students about the dangers of illegal drug use. It has provided billions of dollars to support state and local drug-prevention programs, and required that schools receiving federal funds under the Safe and Drug-Free Schools and Communities Act of 1994 certify that their drug prevention programs "convey a clear and consistent message that . . . the illegal use of drugs [is] wrong and harmful."

## An Appropriate Restriction of Speech

Thousands of school boards throughout the country—including JDHS—have adopted policies aimed at effectuating this message. Those school boards know that peer pressure is perhaps "the single most important factor leading schoolchildren to take drugs," and that students are more likely to use drugs when the norms in school appear to tolerate such behavior [*Earls*]. Student speech celebrating illegal drug use at a school event, in the presence of school administrators and teachers, thus poses a particular challenge for school officials working to protect those entrusted to their care from the dangers of drug abuse.

The "special characteristics of the school environment" [*Tinker*], and the governmental interest in stopping student drug abuse—reflected in the policies of Congress and myriad school boards, including JDHS—allow schools to restrict student expression that they reasonably regard as promoting illegal drug use. *Tinker* warned that schools may not prohibit student speech because of "undifferentiated fear or apprehension of disturbance" or "a mere desire to avoid the discomfort and unpleasantness that always accompany an unpopular viewpoint." The danger here is far more serious and palpable. The particular concern to prevent student drug abuse at issue here, embodied in established school policy, extends well beyond an abstract desire to avoid controversy. . . .

School principals have a difficult job, and a vitally important one. When Frederick suddenly and unexpectedly unfurled his banner, Morse had to decide to act—or not act—on the spot. It was reasonable for her to conclude that the banner promoted illegal drug use—in violation of established school policy—and that failing to act would send a powerful message to the students in her charge, including Frederick, about how serious the school was about the dangers of illegal drug use. The First Amendment does not require schools to tolerate at school events student expression that contributes to those dangers.

# CHAPTER 4

# What Are Some Concerns About Teen Privacy and New Technology?

# Overview: Children, Privacy, and Online Social Networks

*Federal Trade Commission*

*The US Federal Trade Commission is a federal agency that oversees consumer protection and competition jurisdiction in broad sectors of the economy.*

"*It's 10 p.m. Do you know where your children are?*"

Remember that phrase from your own childhood? It's still a valid question, but now, it comes with a twist: "Do you know where your kids are—and who they're chatting with online?"

## The Risks of Social Networking

Social networking sites have morphed into a mainstream medium for teens and adults. These sites encourage and enable people to exchange information about themselves, share pictures and videos, and use blogs and private messaging to communicate with friends, others who share interests, and sometimes even the world at large. And that's why it's important to be aware of the possible pitfalls that come with networking online.

Some social networking sites attract preteens—even kids as young as 5 or 6. These younger-focused sites don't allow the same kinds of communication that teens and adults have, but there are still things that parents can do to help young kids socialize safely online. In fact, when it comes to young kids, the law provides some protections—and gives parents some control over the type of information that children can disclose online. For sites directed to children under age 13,

Federal Trade Commission, "Social Networking Sites: A Parent's Guide," *FTC Facts for Consumers*, September 2007. www.ftc.gov.

and for general audience sites that know they're dealing with kids younger than 13, there's the Children's Online Privacy Protection Act (COPPA). It requires these sites to get parental consent before they collect, maintain, or use kids' information. COPPA also allows parents to review their child's online profiles and blog pages.

Parents sometimes can feel outpaced by their technologically savvy kids. Technology aside, there are lessons that parents can teach to help kids stay safer as they socialize online.

## Keeping Information Private

The Federal Trade Commission, the nation's consumer protection agency, urges parents to talk to their tweens and teens about social networking sites, and offers these tips for using these sites safely:

- Help your kids understand what information should be private. Tell them why it's important to keep some things—about themselves, family members and friends—to themselves. Information like their full name, Social Security number, street address, phone number, and family financial information—like bank or credit card account numbers—is private and should stay that way. Tell them not to choose a screen name that gives away too much personal information.

- Use privacy settings to restrict who can access and post on your child's website. Some social networking sites have strong privacy settings. Show your child how to use these settings to limit who can view their online profile, and explain to them why this is important.

- Explain that kids should post only information that you—and they—are comfortable with others seeing. Even if privacy settings are turned on, some—or even all—of your child's profile may be seen by a broader audience than you're comfortable with. Encourage your child to think about the language used in a blog, and to think before posting pictures and videos. Employers, college admissions officers, team coaches, and teachers may view your child's postings. Even a kid's screen name could make a difference. Encourage teens to think about the impression that screen names could make.

- Remind your kids that once they post information online, they can't take it back. Even if they delete the information from a site, older versions may exist on other people's computers and may be circulated online.

## Teen Behavior Online

- Know how your kids are getting online. More and more, kids are accessing the Internet through their cell phones. Find out about what limits you can place on your child's cell phone. Some cellular companies have plans that limit downloads, Internet access, and texting; other plans allow kids to use those features only at certain times of day.

- Talk to your kids about bullying. Online bullying can take many forms, from spreading rumors online and posting or forwarding private messages without the sender's OK to sending threatening messages. Tell your kids that the words they type and the images they post can have real-world consequences. They can make the target of the bullying feel bad, make the sender look bad—and, sometimes, can bring on punishment from the authorities. Encourage your kids to talk to you if they feel targeted by a bully.

- Talk to your kids about avoiding sex talk online. Recent research shows that teens who don't talk about sex with strangers online are less likely to come in contact with a predator.

- If you're concerned that your child is engaging in risky online behavior, you can search the blog sites they visit to see what information they're posting. Try searching by their name, nickname, school, hobbies, grade, or area where you live.

- Tell your kids to trust their gut if they have suspicions. If they feel threatened by someone or uncomfortable because of something online, encourage them to tell you. You can then help them report concerns to the police and to the social networking site. Most sites have links where users can immediately report abusive, suspicious, or inappropriate online behavior.

- Read sites' privacy policies. Spend some time with a site's privacy policy, FAQs [frequently asked questions] and parent sections to understand its features and privacy controls. The site should spell out your rights as a parent to review and delete your child's profile if your child is younger than 13.

## Privacy for Preteens

Many of the tips above apply for preteens, but parents of younger children also can:

- Take extra steps to protect younger kids. Keep the computer in an open area like the kitchen or family room, so you can keep an eye on what your kids are doing online. Use the Internet with them to help develop safe surfing habits. Consider taking advantage of parental control features on some operating systems that let you manage your kids' computer use, including what sites they can visit, whether they can download items, or what time of day they can be online.

- Go where your kids go online. Sign up for—and use— the social networking spaces that your kids visit. Let them know that you're there, and help teach them how to act as they socialize online.

- Review your child's friends list. You may want to limit your child's online "friends" to people your child actually knows and is friendly with in real life.

- Understand sites' privacy policies. Sites should spell out your rights as a parent to review and delete your child's profile if your child is younger than 13.

# Teen Privacy Is Threatened by Social Networking

*Peter Bazalgette*

*Peter Bazalgette is nonexecutive chairman for Sony Pictures Television's United Kingdom production business.*

When [leader of the United Kingdom's Conservative Party and prime minister as of May 2010] David Cameron's brush with drugs at Eton [College] was revealed earlier this year [2007] he resolutely refused to comment. The Tory leader justified his stance with a simple phrase: 'Everyone deserves a private past.'

Not long before, another vice of the adolescent Cameron had been unearthed—his membership of the Bullingdon Club at Oxford. A photograph appeared of David and his fellow peacocks to prove it, only to disappear when the photographers selling the image were told how unfair bringing up the past could be. Cameron was at university in the 1980s, before the advent of MySpace, Bebo, Facebook and all the other confessional media that have mushroomed in the last five years.

## A Generation with Little Privacy

Imagine how different it will be for the politicians of the future who are at school or university today. The bulk of them use their MySpace and Facebook entries for self-advertisement, social networking and the generally raw process of growing up and working out their identities. With the aid of these sites, they are the first generation who can tell you precisely how many 'friends' they have. They are also the first generation whose sexual adventures, drug taking, immature opinions and personal photographs are indelibly recorded electronically.

Peter Bazalgette, "Your Honour, It's About Those Facebook Photos of You at 20 . . . ," *Observer* (UK), May 20, 2007. Reproduced by permission.

Can you truly delete entries from social networking sites with the confidence they no longer exist on a server somewhere? You cannot. And that is only your entry. Typically, the 'wall' on each site has more than a thousand postings from other users—random, careless remarks recorded for posterity. Indeed, as the drive intensifies by social networking sites to monetise their traffic, they will need to record and preserve the activities of their users with ever-greater accuracy. The sites have declared policies on privacy, but these mostly cover how and whether they use personal data for commercial purposes.

We are a mere three or four years into a wholly new phenomenon: enabled by technology, a generation is voluntarily surrendering its privacy on a hitherto unimaginable scale. I have carried out a highly unscientific straw poll of just one Facebook user. In a five-minute conversation, I asked her for specific instances of personal revelation that might come back to haunt her circle of friends. Here are the results: photographs of marijuana smoking, naked runs and pole dancing; joining anti-women and anti-immigration groups and campaigns to save hereditary peerages (all ironic, but who's to know that in the future?); extreme positions on Israel and Palestine; sexual relationships and confessions. And so it goes on, the normal social banter of students.

Until, that is, it's dug up some years later and given the *Daily Mail* treatment. Already, more astute employers are accessing this material to see what their applicants are really like.

## Attitudes About Privacy

Voluntary self-advertisement of personal details is only part of the story. Recent publicity given to the phenomenon of 'cyberbullying' shows how new technology enables involuntary infringements of privacy, too. Examples where humiliating practical jokes and lewd exposés have been visited on teachers by pupils with video-enabled mobile phones were recently condemned by the Education Secretary. The Italian government took action following a spate of similarly distressing incidents. Among these were the filmed bullying of a disabled child and the sexual harassment of a female teacher. Mobile phones are now banned in Italian schools.

Two interesting issues arise from this explosion of personal electronic traffic. First, is there a fundamental shift taking place in attitudes to privacy? Whether led or merely enabled by the technology, is the famous 'right to be left alone' becoming an outmoded sentiment? If so, there would be profound implications for public policy. And second, even if this generation has a new attitude to privacy, what if they later change their mind? Could their consent subsequently be withdrawn or are the relevant technologies becoming uncontrollable?

---

*To be attracted by self-exposure at a relatively early age does not mean you have no future right to privacy.*

---

To try to gauge how this generation feels about privacy, I commissioned market research company YouGov to carry out a simple survey of attitudes to privacy. The responses it received from a sample group of 2,274 showed that the population as a whole remains very concerned by privacy and easily values it above such qualities as freedom of speech and open access. We also found that while 18- to 24-year-olds prize freedom of speech rather more highly than older generations, even within their own peer group 'privacy' and 'avoiding harm and offence' rate well above freedom of speech and open access.

So, despite the carefree enthusiasm with which some of the younger generation exploit social networking technology, when confronted with some of the dangers, they are almost as concerned as older age groups. I interpret this as a group who loves the powerful social networking that is now possible, but still has a clear sense of privacy. It relates less to a blanket desire for anonymity. We have seen from [television show] *Big Brother* that they are often happy to expose their relationships or, indeed, their flesh.

## The Right to Future Privacy

But they have chosen to do this. My impression is that their idea of privacy is that it should be available if they want it. Some might argue that if you flaunt your private life, you surrender your future right to privacy. I disagree. To be attracted by self-exposure at a relatively early age does not mean you have no future right to privacy. You should be able to change your mind.

Indeed, with the way in which social networking is exploding in popularity among the younger generation, it is essential you should be able to change your mind. The teenagers chattering away online are media literate, but they are not media wise.

This takes us back to the difference between David Cameron at 20 and David Cameron at 40. How, then, should those who run these sites and legislators respond to this new situation?

The [United Kingdom's] Data Protection Act of 1998 was guided by eight principles of good data handling, one of which was that data should not be kept longer than necessary. This could be said to be a precept marked more in the breach than the observance. A new report from the Royal Academy of Engineering has an interesting suggestion: 'Postings to websites might be automatically destroyed after a certain period of time, unless the end user confirmed they wished to have the material retained.'

We need to monitor the attitudes of users—the 'self-advertisers'—in more depth to see if they are truly more open and less private than previous generations. The initial evidence is that they still have an innate sense of privacy. If so, social networking needs to be governed by the same body of law, custom and practice that is developing to protect privacy elsewhere. The key elements would be to increase media literacy, enable the withdrawal of consent and ensure that obsolete data can be effectively deleted.

# Teen Online Activity Can Harm Future College Admissions and Employment

*Nicole Verardi*

*Nicole Verardi is marketing and communications manager at the Association of School Business Officials International.*

You've been working hard trying to get into college—researching schools, refining your essay, collecting glowing recommendations, studying on nights and weekends for the SATs or ACTs, maybe even preparing for a campus interview. Throughout all of this process, you've made a great impression as a serious, promising college student. Wait, though. Before you can relax on the couch to watch *Dancing with the Stars*, and *Glee* on DVR, there's one more detail to take care of—your Facebook profile.

## Social Networking Profiles

Whether it's through Facebook, MySpace, Twitter, YouTube, Flickr or another social media service, students are online—online sharing details with friends, online for everyone to see.

These sites help you keep in touch with friends and allow you to meet new people. Many students spend hours each day updating their profiles, messaging their friends and clicking through photo albums. It's harmless fun, right?

Now, how would you feel if your teachers saw your profile? A college admission officer?

"Well, I would be a little angry because there are things in my profile that I don't want them to see," said Aubrey Fait, a freshman at Saint Mary-of-the-Woods College (IN). "There is some information that I want to keep private between me and

Nicole Verardi, "Social Networking and College Admission," National Association for College Admission Counseling, April 2010. Reproduced by permission.

my friends, so I would prefer if my parents and college faculty not look at my Facebook profile."

Other students don't think what they do in their free time influences their schoolwork, so it shouldn't matter what information they have online. They may be right: You can be a great student, regardless what you do outside of school. When the embarrassing details of your social life are online for anyone to look up, though, you might want to reconsider what you post.

---

*Students in middle school, high school and college are being suspended and expelled for their online indiscretions.*

---

You might not like it, but you should know that adults—from your schools, families and even law enforcement—are looking at your pages.

## The Consequences of Social Networking

Most colleges are not surfing the Web for your profile. However, when other people bring students' blogging to their attention, schools do respond.

- At least one college applicant was denied admission in part because of his blog on LiveJournal. The admission dean said the student's blog, which was brought to his attention, included seemingly hostile comments about certain college officials.

- Swimmers at Louisiana State [University] criticized coaches on Facebook and were kicked off the team.

- A high school freshman in Maryland was reportedly suspended because of online photos.

- Police busted an underage drinking party at George Washington University after they found invitations online.

Many middle and high schools have banned the use of these social networking websites on campus. Some private schools have even banned students from joining these sites altogether.

"I've been on MySpace and I can see that for kids it's like their hangout place, their place to vent, their place to maintain instant contact—it's hard for them to give it up," said Judy Oberlander, a counselor at Ojai Valley School (CA). However, "since MySpace was taking a toll on study time and classroom engagement, in addition to the danger of the imprudent things being posted by students, we decided to outlaw MySpace use at school or any time."

It's happening all across the country: Students in middle school, high school and college are being suspended and expelled for their online indiscretions. Even if you disagree with these policies, they can affect you. And as much of a cliché as it is, your school officials are just trying to protect you.

## The College Admission Effects

With the social networking bans in schools, students need to be careful of what they post. Some zero-tolerance polices make it fair game to punish someone who is in a photo even holding what appears to be an alcoholic drink. Explaining this type of suspension to a college doesn't really make a good bullet point for your resume.

Even if your school doesn't have these rules, your postings could affect your college admission. Most colleges do not look up students on these sites, but when other people draw attention to these possibly offensive blogs, then schools often take action.

"We have just started letting students know that employers, college admission personnel, and others may be checking their postings. . . . Our students seemed very surprised by this," said Julie Davis, Thomas Worthington High School (OH).

"In terms of college admission, I talk with the students about the importance of projecting a professional impression through voice mail messages, e-mail account titles and social media postings. I tell them a story once told to me by an admission counselor who said a student gave her e-mail address as partygirl@hotmail.com. She didn't get accepted to that college," said Margi Wieber, college counselor, Providence Academy (MN).

## The Positive Side of Online Sites

Some college admission officers make themselves available for students on these sites as a convenient forum for Q & A.

"I have accounts on Friendster, Facebook, LiveJournal, Xanga, and MySpace. I do interact with a variety of students via these communities, however, it's our strict policy that the Internet should only help applicants, not hurt them. . . . I, personally, don't think it's fair for college officials to take advantage of [these online interactions]—the one exception being a student's safety," noted Ben Jones, communications manager for the MIT [Massachusetts Institute of Technology] Office of Admissions.

"I don't 'research' applicants online using their pages in these communities—although other schools do, from what I read in the news. My interactions with applicants and current MIT students are initiated by them—not by me."

Jeannine Lalonde, assistant dean of admission at the University of Virginia [UVA], also talks to students online who contact her. "After seeing current UVA students answer questions on MySpace, I decided to step in and offer some advice to the high school students who were posting. I knew it would open the door, but I also knew that seeing an admission officer on MySpace might:

1. Make a few kids stop and think before posting info about questionable behavior on their sites; and

2. Make some students realize that admission officers aren't as scary as they might have thought."

Sometimes students include Web-based communications such as blogs in their college application. Daniel Creasy, from Johns Hopkins University (MD), explains his experiences with student blogs as part of the application: "Many times, the work the students have done adds substance to their file and truly helps, but there have been occasions where this information raises questions and concerns."

Creasy also cautions that when students contact admission officers through the school's message boards and blogs, the information becomes part of the formal correspondence and can be factored into the admission decision.

## Beyond School Impact

Applying to college isn't the only thing you should worry about when you post your information online. Your profile can follow you as you try to get a job.

According to the 2005 study by executive job-search agency ExecuNet cited in the *Chicago Tribune*, 75 percent of recruiters use Web research as part of the applicant screening process.

The same article notes that a recruiter withdrew a job offer after seeing the candidate's blog.

---

*Whatever you post, it never goes away.*

---

One recent grad took down his profile when someone called him about a friend he went to school with. The caller identified himself as an employee at a consulting firm who was "Facebooking" all the applicants and contacting their friends to check them out.

An intern was fired when the CEO [chief executive officer] discovered that the intern's Facebook profile noted that he would "'spend most of [his] days screwing around on IM [instant messaging] and talking to [his] friends and getting paid for it."

There's even a verb for people who get fired for what they put on their websites—*dooced*—named after the blog of a woman who was fired for writing about her job in her blog.

Basically, the point is that whatever you post, it never goes away. Once your information is online—even if you take it down—it becomes public information, as your page can be saved on anyone's computer.

## Steps to Protect Privacy

- First, be safe! Never post personal information such as your address, daily schedule, phone number, etc. Check out these safety guidelines from the Center for Safe and Responsible Internet Use and WiredSafety.

- Make your profile private so that strangers can't look at your information, and be cautious about adding new friends who you do not personally know.

- Take down any questionable photos or exchanges between you and your friends. Give it the "Grandma Test." If you wouldn't want your grandmother to see it, then you don't want other adults to either. Remember, pictures and references of you on your friends' pages can be damaging too. You can ask them to take down this kind of information.

- Don't get a false sense of security on social media sites. It's easy for faculty, alumni and random people to get on and look at the information you have posted.

Although social networking can be fun, remember that sometimes what you post will be in public view, like broadcasting it on the six o'clock news. So when it's time to apply for college, give your social networking profiles a second look to make sure you feel comfortable sharing everything you have posted with an admission officer and, later, with potential employers because your site becomes permanent, public information about you.

# Teen Sexting Can Have Serious Consequences

*Joshua D. Herman*

*Joshua D. Herman is an attorney in Peoria, Illinois, where he represents local governments and educational institutions.*

One in five teenagers has sent sexually suggestive, nude or seminude "sext" messages by phone or otherwise. This [viewpoint] discusses the high-stakes legal issues raised by sexting and their implications for counsel to teens, parents, and schools.

## The Issue of Teen Sexting

"Sexting" is a word you have probably heard but might not be able to define. For purposes of this [viewpoint], "sexting" is the practice of sending nude or seminude pictures by cell phone or other electronic media; it is a sexual text ("sext") message. Sexting is a recent phenomenon, fueled by widespread availability of affordable mobile phones with picture-taking and sending capabilities.

It is increasingly common, especially among sexually curious, hormone-driven teenagers. On average, one in five teens has sent or posted nude or seminude pictures or videos of themselves. Although just over two-thirds of those teens meant those images for their boyfriend or girlfriend, 25 percent of teen girls and 33 percent of teen boys admit they have had sext messages meant for someone else shared with them.

Among teens, sexting is ordinary and somewhat accepted, even though a majority of teens know sexting "can have serious negative consequences." Most, however, do not know it is a crime.

Joshua D. Herman, "Sexting: It's No Joke, It's a Crime," *Illinois Bar Journal*, vol. 98, no. 4, April 2010, p. 192. Reproduced by permission.

Adults risk embarrassment if their sext message is misdirected. But when a teenager (meaning a minor between 13 and 17) creates, sends, or receives a sext message in Illinois, he or she may have committed the criminal offense of child pornography. Sex offense laws predating the sexting phenomenon do not contemplate the ease and frequency with which teens send risqué pictures to each other from their phones. Nonetheless, they subject sexting teens to a myriad of felony charges and branding as a "sex offender."

A teenager's ability to snap a picture and send it in seconds without reflection gives rise to new legal issues for society and the legal community. Teen sexting confronts attorneys and courts with new and complicated legal issues. Across the nation, prosecutors and police are not yet uniform in applying these laws to the minors they were meant to protect. Criminal and juvenile courts must also ponder applying severe criminal penalties to youth who may have merely had a moment of poor judgment.

Moreover, a sexting teen's social and legal problems often converge at the schoolhouse door. For attorneys who counsel educational institutions, it is only a matter of time before they must grapple with sexting-related issues.

These issues pose difficult challenges for school administrators and staff, especially where improper investigation can subject school personnel to prosecution for the same criminal offenses that teens risk by sexting. By being aware of the relevant law and having policies in place to deal with sexting, prosecutors and law enforcement, school districts, parents, and teenagers themselves can curb sexting behavior while avoiding liability.

## The Crime of Sexting

Sexting can have serious social and emotional consequences for teens and adults alike—especially where a picture is taken without knowledge, forwarded without consent, or used to bully and harass. Further, the embarrassment of uncontrolled dissemination of personal and private pictures can significantly disrupt the teen's life.

---

*A 17-year-old who snaps his or her own revealing picture has technically created child pornography.*

---

For example, after hundreds of people were sent sext messages a teen had sent only to her boyfriend, she was cruelly harassed through MySpace and Facebook, leading her to hang herself. In addition to risking reputation and self-esteem, sexting teenagers also expose themselves, their peers, and their school administrators to significant criminal liability.

Most alarmingly, a sexting minor, or a recipient of a sext message from a minor, may have committed one or more felonies under the Illinois child pornography act.... Offenses under the act are generally Class 1 felonies, punishable by fines ranging from $1,000 to $100,000 and imprisonment for four to 15 years.

## The Offense of Child Pornography

In Illinois, a person commits the offense of child pornography by *videotaping or photographing* anyone he or she should know is under the age of 18 and who is engaged in any sexual act or in any pose involving lewd exhibition of unclothed or transparently clothed genitals, pubic area, buttocks, or female breast. *There is no exception for taking pictures of oneself.* Thus, a 17-year-old who snaps his or her own revealing picture has technically created child pornography, a Class 1 felony with a mandatory fine of between $2,000 and $100,000 and at least four years in prison. It would not be a crime if the teen were 18.

*Soliciting or enticing* someone one should know is under the age of 18 to appear in such a picture or videotape is also a child pornography offense. Thus, a 16-year-old boy violates the act if he asks his 16-year-old girlfriend to send him a semi-naked picture. If the youth is 17 or older and uses the Internet to solicit the sext message from a minor, he or she may also be charged with "indecent solicitation of a child," a Class 4 felony.

Forwarding a sext message to others may also constitute the offense of child pornography. *Reproducing or disseminating* such pictures of a person one should know is under the age of 18 is an offense of child pornography. A teen who sends his or her *own picture* to another also violates this provision.

A person who, knowing its content or nature, *possesses* a photograph or film depicting someone he or she should know is under 18 has also violated the act. If the possession is involuntary, the possessor has a defense. Possession is voluntary where a person "knowingly procures or receives" the illicit material "with sufficient time to terminate his or her possession of it."

While the statute does not define "sufficient time," sooner is better than later. Finding and deleting an unsolicited sext message an hour after its receipt better demonstrates involuntary possession than does carrying a sext message on the phone for two months or more.

The act dictates that cell phones used for sexting by minors must be *seized and forfeited*, allowing "law enforcement or prosecuting officers" to possess offending materials as part of the "performance of [their] official duties." School administrators get no such protection when investigating incidents of sexting among students. Consequently, school officials must investigate sexting cautiously because, like teens, they may also be charged with possessing child pornography.

Further, minors who sext across state lines (by using the Internet, for example), or by using materials that traveled in interstate commerce, are also subject to federal charges of child pornography. For example, students who post prohibited pictures on their Facebook pages have likely violated federal criminal law.

## The Risk of Becoming a Sex Offender

In Illinois, someone who commits the offense of child pornography is a "sex offender" and must register and report as such. Not only is noncompliance with reporting a felony, but even compliant individuals face the shame and scrutiny of public reporting.

---

*Some states have attempted to decriminalize sexting among teens, or at least reduce the offense from felony to misdemeanor.*

---

Beyond registering and reporting as sex offenders, students convicted of child pornography may also be bound by other restrictions that can significantly complicate their lives. For example, child sex offenders 17 and older cannot be present on school grounds or loiter or reside within 500 feet of the school building. Revealing that these laws do not contemplate schoolchildren, there are exceptions for sex offenders who are *parents* of students, allowing them to be on school grounds in particular circumstances, but no such exception exists for *student* sex offenders.

The following example places the foregoing offenses in perspective: a 16-year-old girl who snaps a sexual, seminude picture of herself to send as a phone message to her boyfriend has committed at least three felonies by creating, disseminating, and possessing "child pornography." If her boyfriend requested she send the sext message, he is subject to at least two felonies: soliciting and voluntarily possessing the sext message. Thus, one unwise youthful indiscretion results in five felonies and subjects the teenage couple to branding as "sex offenders."

Some states have attempted to decriminalize sexting among teens, or at least reduce the offense from felony to misdemeanor. For example, Vermont recently enacted a law making a teenager's first "sexting" offense a juvenile court matter, giving the teen the opportunity to be sent to a diversionary program rather than be charged as an adult and branded a sex offender.

As this [viewpoint] went to press, the Illinois Senate had just passed SB 2513, which would transform most sexting between teens from a felony to a noncrime by treating the teen in question as a nondelinquent minor in need of supervision under the Juvenile Court Act. Enacting this bill or one like it into law would be a huge step in the right direction. [SB 2513 was still unsigned as of July 2010.]

## Solving the Sexting Problem

Cell phones have become ubiquitous among students, but the law has been slow to catch up. Illinois legislators should continue to examine incidents of sexting and how the current law applies to them. Legislators should consider drafting a narrow exception to sex offenses to prevent "innocent" teens from being charged with serious violations while maintaining liability for those who are guilty of actual child pornography—regardless of age.

Until then, parents and schools may be better equipped to discipline and admonish sexting teens than are police and prosecutors. Because of their age, a vast majority of sexting teenagers attend school. Thus, even if the likelihood that sexting teens will be charged with a felony is remote, school districts cannot ignore the disruptive and potentially tragic consequences of sexting among their students.

School districts should work with local law enforcement in establishing district policies and procedures for investigating allegations of sexting. They should discuss whether and how, if at all, law enforcement will be involved in sexting issues. Because determining what constitutes criminal "child pornography" can be difficult even for those in law enforcement, Dave Haslett, chief of the Illinois Attorney General's High Tech Crimes Bureau, suggests that schools involve law enforcement early to avoid missteps.

## Sexting in School

Based on this dialogue with law enforcement, the school district should revise its policy and procedure accordingly. Additionally, school districts should educate their students about the pitfalls and criminal consequences of sexting.

Naturally, prohibiting student use of cell phones during the school day can greatly reduce sexting issues at school. Because students may still use computers to send, request, or view offending material, school districts should also consider a broader policy prohibiting the creation, possession, or dissemination of obscene or profane materials by students, regardless of the device(s) used.

A school should confirm whether a student alleged to have sexted actually violated school policy. Establishing improper conduct will be easier where the district has explicitly defined inappropriate behavior with regard to sexting in its prohibited conduct policy.

According to attorney Daniel Spillman of the Illinois Attorney General's High Tech Crimes Bureau, possession of a sext message that is child pornography is no different than possessing a "kilo of cocaine." He advises school administrators to immediately confiscate devices with such material on them and report the incident to law enforcement immediately.

Beyond reducing school district exposure, confiscating the device containing the sext message will prevent further dissemination, further harm to any victims, and allow for an investigation of other students that may have been involved or harmed. Involving law enforcement early will also minimize any potential criminal liability of school personnel.

The student pictured in a sext message may be unaware of his or her victimization. Schools should consider when and how they should inform such a student, giving thought to the sensitive nature of the subject and the student's right to privacy. Schools may also consider coordinating this task with local law enforcement and guidance counselors.

Administrators should establish a uniform method for disciplining students involved in sexting. When disciplining sexting students, school personnel should consider the facts of the situation and review district policies related to sexual harassment, bullying, indecent or profane materials, use of electronic devices, and failures to abide by student handbook guidelines.

## Educating Teens and Families

The school district should educate students and parents about sexting and school policies related to the behavior. Many teens, even if they do not sext, consider it "normal" and do not understand sexting is a crime. Many parents are unaware of the phenomenon's pervasiveness or its consequences.

Families should discuss the legal and moral issues surrounding sexting. Parents should frequently review their child's social media, e.g., messages on cell phones, Facebook, MySpace, etc., and set rules for the use of such media. Teenagers and their families should also review their school's policies related to electronic devices and prohibited student conduct.

Teens should not create, possess, solicit, or send/forward sext messages. Teens possessing such messages *involuntarily* have a defense. To ensure the efficacy of this defense, teens must be vigilant in discovering and deleting sext messages.

Lawyers counseling a minor accused of sexting and violating child pornography laws should also consider the minor's role in the creation, dissemination, or possession of the offending material to appreciate potential exposure to other criminal charges. Lawyers should also explore whether a teen's actions give rise to civil liability for claims such as invasion of privacy or defamation.

Finally, although child pornography laws generally regard minors as the victim, prosecuting sexting teens for a strict-liability child pornography offense may be punishing them for their age rather than the content of a sext. Thus, lawyers should also consider whether the content of a sext message constitutes child pornography or is protected speech under the First Amendment.

On average, one in every five teens at a school near you is sexting. Until the Illinois General Assembly amends the criminal code to account for the unforeseen teenage use of technology in violation of the law, sexting will continue to be an increasing social and legal problem. Thus, prosecutors and attorneys for these sexting teens, their parents, and their school districts should be prepared to educate and advise their clients about the social and legal ramifications of sexting.

# The Legal System Is Overly Harsh Toward Teen Sexting

*Radley Balko*

*Radley Balko is a senior editor at* Reason *magazine and Reason .com.*

That the 3rd U.S. Circuit Court of Appeals would even need to hear oral arguments in the case of *Miller et al. v. Skumanick* last week [January 15, 2010] is a pretty good indication that law enforcement officials in Wyoming County, Pennsylvania, have lost their collective minds.

At issue in the case: whether the U.S. Constitution permits prosecutors to charge minors who pose for nude or risqué photos with child pornography. You read that correctly. In order to protect children from predators and child pornographers, the local district attorney is threatening to prosecute minors who pose for racy photos *as if they were* child pornographers.

## An Outlandish Case

Even within the context of the already hysterical overreaction to the "sexting" phenomenon, the facts in *Miller* are jaw-dropping. Of the three girls bringing suit, two were photographed at a slumber party wearing training bras. The third photographed herself baring her breasts, then sent the photo to a boy she'd hoped to make jealous. The girls aren't in trouble for distributing the photos, or even for taking them. They've been introduced to the criminal justice system merely for appearing in them.

Wyoming County District Attorney George Skumanick, Jr. gave the girls a choice. The first option was to face felony

Radley Balko, "Ruining Kids in Order to Save Them," *Reason*, January 25, 2010. Reproduced by permission.

child pornography charges, punishable by up to 10 years in prison. The second was to attend a series of Skumanick-chosen classes, which according to the Pennsylvania ACLU [American Civil Liberties Union] included topics such as "what it means to be a girl in today's society" and "nontraditional societal and job roles." The girls would also be put on probation, subject to random drug tests, and would have to write essays explaining why appearing in photos while wearing their bras is wrong.

Skumanick would later tell a gathering of students and parents that he had the authority to prosecute girls photographed on the beach in bikinis, because the minors would be dressed "provocatively." He told the *Wall Street Journal* that by offering the girls the classes and probation instead of immediately hitting them with felony charges, "We thought we were being progressive."

---

*The message to minors: These photos can ruin your lives, kids. And just to prove it, we're going to ruin your lives.*

---

Of the 19 minors Skumanick targeted, 16 chose the classes. The other three took Skumanick to court, where they won a restraining order. Skumanick appealed. To the credit of the people of Wyoming County, after 20 years in office Skumanick lost his bid for reelection last November. But his office continues to fight. [The court held that there was no legal basis for child pornography charges.]

## Ruining Teen Lives

But this isn't just an isolated case of a renegade D.A. [district attorney]. There have now been several cases across the country where young people who either pose for, snap, or forward provocative or nude photos of other minors are being charged or threatened with felony child pornography. In 2007, a state appeals court in Florida upheld charges of "directing or promoting a photograph featuring the sexual conduct of a child" and possession of child pornography charges against a 17-year-old boy and a 16-year-old girl for forwarding explicit photos of themselves having sex from her computer to his e-mail address. The sex wasn't illegal. But the photos were. Incredibly, Judge James Wolf wrote in the majority opinion that "Mere production of these videos or pictures may . . . result in psychological trauma to the teenagers involved. Further, if these pictures are ultimately released, future damage may be done to these minors' careers or personal lives."

The message to minors: These photos can ruin your lives, kids. And just to prove it, we're going to ruin your lives.

## Two Recent Trends

These cases are the natural culmination of two trends. The first is the continuing view among politicians that there's no punishment too severe for sex offenders. Moreover, to show how serious we are about sex offenders, we should broaden the class of people we classify under the label. And there needn't be any actual victims.

---

*It isn't exactly clear from what or whom the authorities are protecting these teens.*

---

In 2006, Karen Fletcher, also of Pennsylvania, was convicted in federal court for writing *fictional* stories (and granted, they *were* disturbing stories) about sexual and violent crimes against children. Until it was struck down by the Supreme Court in 2002, the 1996 Child Online Protection Act criminalized images of adults made to look like minors, as well as digitally manufactured photos of minors who don't actually exist.

The second trend is the "for the children" excuse that no law ought to be questioned if its intent is to protect young people. The resulting paternalism is built in.

Put these together, and you get the intellectually vacant policy of prosecuting children for sexually exploiting *themselves* . . . in order to protect them from the people who might exploit them.

It isn't exactly clear from what or whom the authorities are protecting these teens. To my knowledge, there hasn't been a single case of a predator who tracked down, then raped, killed, or otherwise physically harmed a minor after viewing explicit photos of the child on the Internet or via images forwarded by cell phone. Perhaps it has happened. But given the media obsession with these stories, if it's happened with any frequency at all, we would have probably heard about it by now.

## The Harm Argument

The harm here seems to be the possibility that somewhere, someone other than the intended recipient of these photos may be masturbating to them. That's an uncomfortable thought, sure. But it's difficult to see how that presents tangible harm to the minors in the photos, certainly not to the point where the minors themselves ought to be prosecuted. Anyone turned on by the photos in Skumanick's case could just as easily placate themselves with an old Sears catalog— and with no resulting damage to the models who posed in it.

But the idea that an otherwise innocuous image can mutate into illegal child porn based on how it might be used by pedophiles is gaining currency. In 2006, Alabama photographer Jeff Pierson was indicted on federal child porn charges for a website he ran featuring aspiring teen models. None of the models were nude, nor were any depicted engaged in any sexual activity. All of the models' parents signed off on the photos. But federal prosecutors argued the models struck "illegally provocative," "lascivious," and "coy" poses that could entice pedophiles. In 2002, Republican Rep. Mark Foley of Florida (yes, *that* Mark Foley) introduced the Child Modeling

Exploitation Prevention Act, which would have prohibited the sale of *any* photo of a minor. It failed, but crazy as Foley's bill sounds, it at least would have cleared up the ambiguity. As the website CNET reported in a story about Pierson, federal courts have made the definition of child porn so subjective, "judges and juries [are] faced with the difficult task of making distinctions between lawful and unlawful camera angles and facial expressions."

## Overreactive Criminal Charges

When applied to "sexting" cases, that also leaves prosecutors like Skumanick far too much leeway—enough, for example, for him to believe he can prosecute a girl photographed in a bikini because *he* finds the photo uncomfortably "provocative." But even when "sexted" photos are unquestionably explicit, there's no justification for criminal charges. Even the deterrent argument falls flat. Despite these high-profile cases, threats of prosecution, and public service announcements on MTV, surveys suggest that about 20–25 percent of young people college-aged and younger have taken or sent explicit photos of themselves. That number is rising, not falling.

The root disconnect, here, is that the law treats prepubescent sex crimes on par with crimes related to teenagers who are sexually mature. Fact is, teenagers become sexually mature years before it's socially or legally permissible to think about them that way. That they're then having sex is nothing new. Nor is the fact that teens make rash, emotional, spur-of-the-moment decisions. What's new is that they're able to document it all in ways that can quickly escape their control. What they need after the fact are responsible adults who can walk them through a poor decision, appropriately reprimand or punish them if necessary, but all while keeping things in perspective, and minimizing the long-term consequences for the teen. Dumping the kid into the criminal justice system has all the subtlety and precision of dropping an anvil on the problem from 40 stories above.

# Organizations to Contact

*The editors have compiled the following list of organizations concerned with the issues debated in this book. The descriptions are derived from materials provided by the organizations. All have publications or information available for interested readers. The list was compiled on the date of publication of the present volume; the information provided here may change. Be aware that many organizations take several weeks or longer to respond to inquiries, so allow as much time as possible.*

**Advocates for Youth**
2000 M Street NW, Suite 750, Washington, DC  20036
(202) 419-3420 • fax: (202) 419-1448
website: www.advocatesforyouth.org

Advocates for Youth is an organization that works both in the United States and in developing countries with a sole focus on adolescent reproductive and sexual health. Advocates for Youth champions efforts that help young people make informed and responsible decisions about their reproductive and sexual health through its core values of Rights, Respect, and Responsibility. Advocates for Youth publishes numerous informational essays available at its website, including "Emergency Contraception: A Safe & Effective Contraceptive Option for Teens."

**American Civil Liberties Union (ACLU)**
125 Broad Street, 18th floor, New York, NY  10004
(212) 549-2500
e-mail: infoaclu@aclu.org
website: www.aclu.org

The American Civil Liberties Union (ACLU) is a national organization that works to defend Americans' civil rights as guaranteed in the US Constitution. The ACLU works in courts, legislatures, and communities to defend First Amendment rights, the right to equal protection, the right to due process, and the right to privacy. The ACLU publishes the semiannual newsletter *Civil Liberties Alert* as well briefing papers, including "Preventing Teenagers from Getting Contraceptives Unless They Tell a Parent Puts Teens at Risk."

## Center for Public Education

1680 Duke Street, Alexandria, VA   22314
(703) 838-6722 • fax: (703) 548-5613
e-mail: centerforpubliced@nsba.org
website: www.centerforpubliceducation.org

The Center for Public Education is a resource center set up by the National School Boards Association (NSBA). The Center for Public Education works to provide information about public education, leading to more understanding about our schools, more community-wide involvement, and better decision making by school leaders on behalf of all students in their classrooms. Among the many publications available at the center's website is "Search and Seizure, Due Process, and Public Schools."

## Center for Reproductive Rights

120 Wall Street, New York, NY   10005
(917) 637-3600 • fax: (917) 637-3666
e-mail: info@reprorights.org
website: www.reproductiverights.org

The Center for Reproductive Rights is a global legal advocacy organization dedicated to reproductive rights. The center uses the law to advance reproductive freedom as a fundamental human right that all governments are legally obligated to protect, respect, and fulfill. The Center for Reproductive Rights publishes articles, reports, and briefing papers, among which is the article "Parental Involvement Laws."

## Guttmacher Institute

125 Maiden Lane, 7th floor, New York, NY   10038
(212) 248-1111 • fax: (212) 248-1951
website: www.agi-usa.org

The Guttmacher Institute works to advance sexual and reproductive health worldwide through an interrelated program of social science research, public education, and policy analysis. The Guttmacher Institute collects and analyzes scientific evidence to make a difference in policies, programs, and medical practice. The institute's monthly *State Policies in Brief* provides information on legislative and judicial actions affecting reproductive health, including the recent brief "An Overview of Minors' Consent Laws."

## Internet Education Foundation

1634 I Street NW, Suite 1100, Washington, DC   20006
(202) 638-4370 • fax: (202) 637-0968
e-mail: tim@neted.org
website: www.neted.org

The Internet Education Foundation is a nonprofit organization dedicated to educating the public and policy makers about the Internet. The Internet Education Foundation works to educate the public about the challenges and problems presented online. One of the foundation's projects is GetNetWise (www.getnetwise.org), an online portal with information regarding child safety, online privacy, and security issues on the Internet.

## National Right to Life Committee (NRLC)

512 Tenth Street NW, Washington, DC   20004
(202) 626-8800
e-mail: nrlc@nrlc.org
website: www.nrlc.org

The National Right to Life Committee (NRLC) was established after the decision in *Roe v. Wade* (1973), to repeal the right to abortion. The NRLC works toward legislative reform at the national level to restrict abortion. NRLC publishes a monthly newspaper, the *National Right to Life News*, and several fact sheets, including "Teens and Abortion: Why Parents Should Know."

## Student Drug-Testing Institute (SDTI)

8757 Georgia Avenue, Suite 1440, Silver Spring, MD   20910
(866) 956-SDTI (7384)
e-mail: SDTI@seiservices.com
website: http://sdti.ed.gov

The US Department of Education's Student Drug-Testing Institute (SDTI) provides information on many aspects of student drug testing programs. The institute supports school efforts to implement student drug testing (SDT) programs by recommending the necessary components of developing an SDT program, implementing a confidential and effective program, and sustaining a program to promote drug-free students. Among the resources available at its website are publications about drug testing programs and links to studies about drug testing.

# Bibliography

## Books

William P. Bloss — *Under a Watchful Eye: Privacy Rights and Criminal Justice.* Santa Barbara, CA: Praeger, 2009.

Kenneth Dautrich, David A. Yalof, and Mark Hugo Lopez — *The Future of the First Amendment: The Digital Media, Civic Education, and Free Expression Rights in America's High Schools.* Lanham, MD: Rowman & Littlefield Publishers, 2008.

Maureen T.B. Drysdale and B.J. Rye, eds. — *Taking Sides: Clashing Views in Adolescence.* Dubuque, IA: McGraw-Hill, 2006.

David H. Holtzman — *Privacy Lost: How Technology Is Endangering Your Privacy.* San Francisco, CA: Jossey-Bass, 2006.

Jon L. Mills — *Privacy: The Lost Right.* New York: Oxford University Press, 2008.

Kathryn C. Montgomery — *Generation Digital: Politics, Commerce, and Childhood in the Age of the Internet.* Cambridge, MA: MIT Press, 2007.

John Palfrey and Urs Gasser — *Born Digital: Understanding the First Generation of Digital Natives.* New York: Basic Books, 2008.

Charles J. Russo and Ralph D. Mawdsley
*Searches, Seizures, and Drug-Testing Procedures: Balancing Rights and School Safety*. 2nd ed. Danvers, MA: LRP Publications, 2008.

Gregory S. Smith
*How to Protect Your Children on the Internet: A Roadmap for Parents and Teachers*. Westport, CT: Praeger, 2007.

Janet E. Smith
*The Right to Privacy*. San Francisco, CA: Ignatius Press, 2008.

Daniel J. Solove
*The Future of Reputation: Gossip, Rumor, and Privacy on the Internet*. New Haven, CT: Yale University Press, 2007.

## Periodicals

Stephanie L. Anderson, Judith Schaechter, and Jeffrey P. Brosco
"Adolescent Patients and Their Confidentiality: Staying Within Legal Bounds," *Contemporary Pediatrics*, July 2005.

Michele Bachmann
"Is No Girl Too Young for Plan B?" Townhall.com, April 23, 2009. http://townhall.com.

Karina Bland
"'Sexting' Can Have Serious Consequences," *Arizona Republic*, August 27, 2009.

Larry K. Brendtro and Gordon A. Martin Jr.
"Respect Versus Surveillance: Drug Testing Our Students," *Reclaiming Children and Youth: The Journal of Strength-Based Interventions*, Summer 2006.

Kathryn S. Vander Broek, Steven M. Puiszis, and Evan D. Brown
"Schools and Social Media: First Amendment Issues Arising from Student Use of the Internet," *Intellectual Property & Technology Law Journal*, April 2009.

Michelle Conlin
"You Are What You Post: Bosses Are Using Google to Peer into Places Job Interviews Can't Take Them," *BusinessWeek*, March 27, 2006.

Steve Dennis
"Liberalism, Replacing Parental Rights with Government Control," *America's Watchtower Blog*, October 17, 2007. http://americaswatchtower.com.

Floralynn Einesman and Howard Taras
"Drug Testing of Students: A Legal and Public Health Perspective," *Journal of Contemporary Health Law & Policy*, Spring 2007.

Risa Vetri Ferman and Lynne Abraham
"Sexting: A Fun, Flirtatious Felony," *Mercury* (Pottstown, PA), October 3, 2009.

Nancy Gibbs
"Birth Control for Kids?" *Time*, October 18, 2007.

Rachel Benson Gold
"Unintended Consequences: How Insurance Processes Inadvertently Abrogate Patient Confidentiality," *Guttmacher Policy Review*, Fall 2009.

Jennifer Golson and Joe Ryan
"A Debate Swirls over Teens' Lurid Pictures," *Star-Ledger* (Newark, NJ), March 29, 2009.

Jimmy Greenfield | "All Up in My Space," *Chicago Tribune*, March 28, 2006.

Rebecca Hagelin | "College Students & Privacy: Do Your Homework," Heritage Foundation, November 7, 2007.

Eric Hartley | "Sometimes, Privacy Must Take a Back Seat," *Capital* (Annapolis, MD), June 14, 2009.

Monica Yant Kinney | "Another Pin in the Privacy Balloon," *Philadelphia Inquirer*, February 28, 2010.

Janet Kornblum and Mary Beth Marklein | "What You Say Online Could Haunt You," *USA Today*, March 8, 2006.

Scott Lemieux | "Bypassing Young Women's Abortion Rights," *American Prospect*, August 17, 2007.

Melissa L. Luhtanen and Lisa Ellis | "Youth and Privacy in a Networked World," *LawNow*, May–June 2007.

Linda McKay-Panos | "Privacy in Schools: Dogs, Lockers, Bodies, and Backpacks," *LawNow*, March–April 2009.

Daniel P. Moloney | "Planned Teen Parenthood," *National Review Online*, July 1, 2008.

Ed Morales | "Pentagon Going Too Far with Teen Database," *Progressive*, June 29, 2005.

| | |
|---|---|
| Lucy Morgan | "94% Who Ask Get Abortions," *St. Petersburg Times* (St. Petersburg, FL), October 19, 2006. |
| Michael J. New | "A Parental-Involvement Opportunity," *National Review Online*, September 16, 2008. |
| James Plummer | "Pentagon's Vast Recruiting Database Prompts Privacy Fears," *Human Events*, January 25, 2006. |
| Nancy Rommelmann | "Anatomy of a Child Pornographer," *Reason*, July 2009. |
| Helena Silverstein and Wayne Fishman | "Justice Bypassed," *American Prospect*, July 27, 2006. |
| Bree Sposato | "MySpace Invaders," *New York Magazine*, November 21, 2005. |
| Jacob Sullum | "Fourth Amendment Victory in Advil Strip Search Case," *Reason*, June 25, 2009. |
| Nathan Tabor | "Giving Parents a Break," *Human Events*, July 26, 2006. |
| JoAnn Wypijewski | "Through a Lens Starkly," *Nation*, May 18, 2009. |

# Index

## A

Abortion
  antichoice movement, 52–54
  HIPAA Privacy Rule and, 48
  judicial bypass requirement,
    81
  minors and, 15, 42, 44, 46–47
  parental consent and, 15, 44,
    51–55, 80–83
  pro-choice movement, 55
  rights, 15
Adolescents
  alienation of, 90
  communication with, 54
  confidentiality debate over,
    43–45
  development of, 20, 45–46, 50
  health of, 43, 49, 71, 89
  substance abuse by, 107, 113
  vulnerability of, 98
  *See also* Minors; Teens
Adolescents, privacy rights. *See*
  Teens, privacy rights
Adoption issues, 41
Age distinctions and privacy, 22
Alcohol use/abuse
  family relations and, 23–24
  on social networking sites,
    150–151
  student searches and, 97
  testing for, 90, 112–113
  treatment services for, 40
American Academy of Pediatrics,
  71, 89, 90
American Association of School
  Administrators, 114–125

American Civil Liberties Union
  (ACLU), 166
American Public Health Associa-
  tion, 90
Amphetamine testing, 112
Antichoice movement, 52–54
Association for Addiction Profes-
  sionals, 90

## B

Balko, Radley, 165–169
Barwick, Melanie, 20–25
Bathroom privacy rights, 18, 20,
  23–24, 97
Bazalgette, Peter, 144–148
Bedroom privacy rights, 18, 20,
  23–24
Behavior guidelines
  dangerous behavior risks and,
    89, 107–108
  for health, 46, 50
  on-the-job, 33
  online, 141–142, 152
  rules for, 23–24
  in schools, 122, 136, 162–163
  sexual, 54, 157
Bell, Becky, 51–53, 82
*Bellotti v. Baird*, 15
*Bethel School District No. 403 v.
  Fraser*, 126, 133–134
Birth control. *See* Contraceptives
Blanchard, Jim, 52
Blogs/blogging, 139, 140–142,
  150–151, 153–154
*Board of Education v. Earls*, 110,
  120–121, 136

Breathalyzer testing, 113
*Brinegar v. United States*, 94
Bullying behavior, 23, 26
    *See also* Cyberbullying

## C

Cameron, David, 144, 147
*Carey v. Population Services International*, 14–15, 60
*Carroll v. United States*, 94
Center for Reproductive Rights, 56–60, 61
Centers for Disease Control and Prevention (CDC), 106
*Chicago Tribune*, 153
Child Modeling Exploitation Prevention Act, 168–169
Child Online Protection Act, 167
Child pornography, 157, 158–162, 166–167
Children's Online Privacy Protection Act (COPPA), 140
*Chronicle*, 35–38
Cocaine testing, 112
Colb, Sherry F., 61–67
College admission concerns, 149–155
Condom purchases, 56
Confidential health care
    adolescent development and, 45–46
    debate over, 43–45
    family planning clinics/ services, 46, 49, 59
    federal programs for, 57–58, 73–74
    health insurance and, 48, 69–79
    HIPAA Privacy Rule and, 48, 49–50
    importance of, 47–48

legal support for, 48–49
    Medicaid, 57, 72, 73–75, 78
    rules for, 74–76
    SCHIP, 73–75
    Title X Family Planning program, 49, 57, 71, 73–76, 78
    *See also* Medical privacy
Contraceptives
    access to, 58–59, 70, 85–86
    banning, 14
    condom purchases, 56
    Depo-Provera, 56, 75
    HIPAA Privacy Rule and, 48
    minors and, 41, 56–60, 71, 75
    morning-after pill, 73
    parental consent and, 47, 56–60, 84–86
    right to, 14–15
    school officials and, 90
Council on School Health, 89
Creasy, Daniel, 153
Cyberbullying, 37, 103–104, 141, 145–146

## D

Dangerous behaviors, 89, 107–108
    *See also* Alcohol use/abuse; Drug use/abuse; Sexting
Data Protection Act, 147
Davis, Julie, 151–152
Department of Education (DOE), 91, 109, 112
Depo-Provera contraception, 56, 75
Drug use/abuse
    dangers of, 108, 135–136
    intervention as treatment, 110–111, 123–124
    marijuana use, 89, 106, 112–113, 128–131
    parental consent and, 23–24, 71–73

of prescription drugs, 106, 115, 122–123
of steroids, 106, 112
student searches and, 120–122
by students, 105–107
testing for, 88–91
*See also* Random drug testing; specific drugs

**E**

Earned privacy, 29–31
Ecstasy (MDMA) testing, 112
Emergency contraception, 56
Employment concerns, 23, 153–155
English, Abigail, 43–50
Ethyl glucuronide (EtG) test, 113

**F**

Facebook (online social networking site)
    advantages of, 152
    behavior guidelines for, 23
    employment concerns, 153–155
    future concerns over, 144–145
    parental involvement with, 36
    privacy of, 20, 21, 149
    sexting and, 158, 159, 163
    student speech and, 102, 103
Fait, Aubrey, 149–150
Family Educational Rights and Privacy Act (FERPA), 112
Family involvement, 23–24
Family planning clinics/services, 46, 49, 59, 71
Federal health programs, 57–58, 73–74
    *See also* specific programs
Federal Trade Commission (FTC), 139–143

Ferrier, Lindsay, 32–34
First Amendment rights
    drug use and, 137
    sexting and, 164
    student free speech and, 101–104, 126–127, 129–130, 132–134
Fletcher, Karen, 167
Flickr (online photo site), 149
Foley, Mark, 168–169
Fortas, Abe, 103
Fourth Amendment Rights, 92–95, 98, 114, 120, 134–135
Fraser, Matthew, 133–134
Frederick, Joseph, 127–132, 134, 137
Friendster (online social networking site), 152

**G**

Gamma-hydroxybutyrate (GHB) testing, 112
Glines, Marissa, 93, 96–97, 99–100
Government health programs, 57–58, 73–74
Granju, Katie Allison, 34
*Griswold v. Connecticut*, 14
Guttmacher Institute, 40–42, 58, 75

**H**

Harm issues. *See* Risk/harm issues
Haslett, David, 161
*Hazelwood School District v. Kuhlmeier*, 126, 134–135
Health care. *See* Confidential health care; Medical privacy
Health insurance, 48, 69–79

Health Insurance Portability and Accountability Act (HIPAA), 48, 49–50
Healthy behaviors, 46, 50
Herman, Joshua D., 156–164
High Tech Crimes Bureau, 161, 162
HIPAA Privacy Rule. *See* Health Insurance Portability and Accountability Act
Homework concerns, 29–30

**I**

*Illinois v. Gates,* 95
*In loco parentis,* 15
Incest issues, 54, 66
Institute of Education Sciences, 109
The Internet
    behavior on, 141–142, 152
    blogs/blogging, 139, 140–142, 150–151, 153–154
    college/employment concerns and, 149–155
    cyberbullying, 37, 103–104, 141, 145–146
    employer searches on, 23
    privacy rights of, 36–37
    as private time, 28
    safety tips and, 140–141
    sex talk online, 141
    *See also* Facebook; MySpace; Social networking
Intervention as treatment, 110–111, 123–124

**J**

Johnston, Lloyd, 88
Jones, Ben, 152
*J.S. v. Blue Mountain,* 102

Judicial bypass requirement, 15, 48, 59, 81–83
Juneau-Douglas High School (JDHS), 127, 136
Justified-at-inception analysis, 97, 115–118, 120
Juvenile Court Act, 161

**L**

Lalonde, Jeannine, 152
*Layshock v. Hermitage School District,* 102
*Legal Intelligencer,* 102
LiveJournal (online networking site), 152

**M**

Mandatory reporting laws
    controversy over, 66–67
    harm of, 65–67
    overview, 61–62
    point of, 65
    teenage sex and, 62–64
    victim impact, 64
    *See also* Parental consent
Marijuana use, 89, 106, 112–113, 128–131
Marital privacy rights, 14, 62
Massachusetts Institute of Technology (MIT), 152
Maturation process, 45–46
Meadows, Mikki, 22
Medicaid, 57, 72, 73–75, 78
Medical privacy
    approaches to, 69–70
    confidential health care and, 43–50
    morality of, 70–71
    overview, 40–42, 68–69
    parental rights and, 68–79
    reforms for, 76–78

*See also* Confidential health
care
Meier, Megan, 103–104
Methamphetamine use, 89
Michelman, Kate, 51–55
*Miller et al. v. Skumanick,* 165
Minors
abortion and, 15, 42, 44,
46–47
adoption and, 41
adoption issues and, 41
consent laws for, 16, 40–42,
48–49, 80
contraceptives and, 41, 56–60,
71, 75
defined, 14–15, 157
drug addiction by, 72–73
mandatory reporting laws
and, 61–67
private insurance and, 72, 76
right to privacy, 18, 59–60
SCHIP and, 74
sexting and, 158–159, 161,
165–169
*See also* Adolescents; Confidential health care; Medical
privacy; Parental involvement laws; Preteens; Teens
Moloney, Daniel Patrick, 68–79
Monitoring the Future survey
(2008), 105–106, 123–124
Moral issues, 70–71, 78, 79
Morning-after pill, 73
Morse, Deborah, 127, 129–131,
137
*Morse v. Frederick,* 121
MySpace (online social networking site)
advantages of, 152–153
First Amendment rights and,
102
future concerns over, 144
privacy concerns on, 26–28,
149
school banning of, 151
sexting and, 158, 163

**N**

National Association of Social
Workers, 90
National Council on Alcoholism
and Drug Dependence, 90
National Education Association,
90
National health insurance, 69–71
National Institute on Drug Abuse
(NIDA), 88, 90, 113, 123
National School Boards Associa-
tion, 114–125
National Survey on Drug Use and
Health, 107–108
*New Jersey v. T.L.O.*
school privacy rights, 15–16
student searches, 94, 99–100,
114–120, 135

**O**

Oberlander, Judy, 151
Offcampus speech rights, 101–104
Office of National Drug Control
Policy (ONDCP), 91, 122–123
Office of Safe and Drug-Free
Schools, 109
On-the-job behavior, 33
Online privacy rights. *See* the In-
ternet
*Ornelas v. United States,* 95

**P**

Parental consent
for abortion, 15, 44, 51–55,
80–83

for contraceptives, 47, 56–60,
84–86
dangers of, 51–52
drug use/abuse and, 23–24,
71–73
judicial bypass and, 15, 48, 59,
81–83
*in loco parentis,* 15
social networking and, 36
STDs and, 44
teen communication and,
54–55
*See also* Mandatory reporting
laws
Parental involvement laws
abortion and, 53–54
constitutionality of, 80–81
myth of, 82–83
purpose of, 81
Parents/parenting
adolescent development and,
45–46
family involvement and,
23–24
homework concerns, 29–30
medical privacy rights and,
68–79
relationships with, 33–34
responsibilities of, 37–38, 79,
84–85
rights of, 35–36, 76–79
spying by, 32–33
teen privacy rights, 20–25,
32–34
*Patriot Ledger,* 84–86
Peer pressure, 85, 105, 106–107,
136
Phencyclidine (PCP) testing, 112
Pierson, Jeff, 168
Planned Parenthood, 75
*Planned Parenthood of Central
Missouri v. Danforth,* 15

*Planned Parenthood of Southeast-
ern Pennsylvania v. Casey,* 15
Pregnancy
parental communication and,
51, 54
prenatal care, 40, 41
rates of, 44, 58, 64
*See also* Abortion; Contracep-
tives
Prenatal care, 40, 41
Prescription drug abuse, 106, 115,
122–123
Preteens
privacy rights, 85–86, 142–143
social networking and, 20,
139–140
Prince, Phoebe, 103–104
Private insurance, 72, 76
Private time needs, 26–28
Pro-choice movement, 55
Probable cause requirements,
94–95
Promiscuity, 85
Protection of Pupil Rights
Amendment (PPRA), 112

**Q**

Qualified immunity, 93–94

**R**

Random drug testing
breathalyzer testing, 113
consequences of, 110–111
drug detection and, 112–113
legality of, 109–110
privacy rights with, 111–112
process of, 112
questions about, 107–108
research on, 108–109
student drug use and, 105–
107

Rape issues, 54, 66, 73, 75
Reasonable-in-scope prong, 115–119, 124–125
Redding, Savana, 92–100
Relationships, with parents, 33–34
Risk/harm issues
  behavior guidelines and, 89, 107–108
  incest, 54, 66
  mitigating, 22
  privacy boundary and, 24
  rape, 54, 66, 73, 75
  sex offenders and, 160–161
  social networking, 139–140
  See also Alcohol use/abuse; Drug use/abuse; Sexting
RMC Research, 109
Roberts, John, 126–137
Roe v. Wade, 15, 51, 53
Romero, Helen, 93, 98
Romero, Jordan, 95–96
Royal Academy of Engineering, 147

S

Safe and Drug-Free Schools and Communities Act, 136
Safford Unified School District #1 v. April Redding, 114–115
SCHIP. See State Children's Health Insurance Program
School privacy rights
  behavior guidelines and, 122, 136, 162–163
  homework concerns and, 29–30
  offcampus speech rights, 101–104
  overview, 88–91
  random drug testing and, 105–113

unwarranted searches, 92–100, 114–125
  See also Sexting; Student free speech
Schwallier, Peggy, 93, 96–98
Sexting (sexually suggestive texting)
  as child pornography, 157, 158–162, 166–167
  as criminal offense, 157–158
  education about, 163–164
  harm argument against, 168–169
  issue of, 156–157
  legal trends against, 167–168
  minors and, 158–159, 161, 165–169
  overreaction to, 165–166, 169
  in school, 162–163
  sex offender risk and, 160–161
  solutions for, 161
Sexual behavior
  abuse/assault, 62–64, 90
  guidelines, 54, 157
  online, 141
  promiscuity, 85
  rape issues and, 54, 66, 73, 75
  view of, 62–63
Sexual orientation counseling, 73
Sexually transmitted diseases (STDs)
  increases in, 47
  minors' consent and, 41
  parental consent and, 44
  spread of, 65
  testing for, 76
Silverman, Justin, 101–104
Skumanick, George, Jr., 165–166, 168
Smith, Mailee R., 80–83
Social networking
  advantages of, 152–153
  attitudes about, 145–147

college admissions and, 151–152

consequences of, 150–151

cyberbullying and, 145–146

employment concerns over, 23, 153–155

on Flickr, 149

on Friendster, 152

future concerns over, 144–145, 147–148

on LiveJournal, 152

online, 139–143

by parents, 20–21

privacy rights, 144–148

profiles on, 149–150

risks of, 139–140

safety tips for, 140–141, 154

on Twitter, 149

on YouTube, 23, 149

*See also* Facebook; MySpace

Souter, David, 92–100

Spear, Scott J., 43–50

Spillman, Daniel, 162

Spying, by parents, 32–33

State Children's Health Insurance Program (SCHIP), 72–75, 78

Steroid use, 106, 112

Student Drug-Testing Institute, 105–113

Student free speech

Facebook and, 102, 103

First Amendment rights, 101–104, 126–127, 129–130, 132–133, 132–134

Fourth Amendment rights, 134–135

interpretation of, 131–132

latitude over, 134–135

offcampus rights, 101–104, 126–137

offensiveness of, 130–131

restrictions of, 132–133, 136–137

school interest in, 135–136

school-sanctioned, 126–127

school suspension over, 127–128

Student searches

deference to educators in, 119–120

drug abuse and, 120–122

drug concerns and, 95–96

educator guidelines for, 119

Fourth Amendment rights and, 92–95, 98, 114, 120

gender issues, 119

intervention and, 123–124

as intrusive, 99–100

justified-at-inception analysis, 97, 114–115, 117–118

limits of, 100

prescription/OTC drugs and, 122–123

privacy issues and, 97–99

probable cause requirements, 94–95

reasonable-in-scope prong, 115–119, 124–125

sliding scale approach to, 117–118

suspicions needed, 116–117

*T.L.O.* test for, 114–116

Students for Sensible Drug Policy, 88–91

Substance abuse. *See* Alcohol use/abuse; Drug use/abuse

Suicide concerns, 23, 24, 73, 103–104

Supreme Court (U.S.) cases

abortion and, 48

contraception and, 14–15, 59–60

drug testing and, 91, 110

First Amendment rights and, 126–127

justified-at-inception and, 97, 115–118, 120

parental involvement laws and, 80–81

privacy controversies and, 16

student searches and, 120–122

student speech and, 101–102

*See also* specific cases

# T

Taras, Howard, 89

Teens

communication with, 54–55

peer pressure, 85, 105, 106–107, 136

pregnancy among, 47, 55, 58

suicide among, 23, 24, 73, 103–104

*See also* Adolescents; Minors

Teens, privacy rights

from adults, 26–28

age distinctions and, 22

in bathrooms, 18, 20, 23–24, 97

in bedrooms, 18, 20, 23–24

controversy over, 14, 18–19, 34

as earned, 29–31

invasion of, 35–38

marriage and, 14, 62

moral issues of, 70–71, 78, 79

from parents, 20–25, 32–34

respecting, 24–25

sex and, 62–63

for social networking, 144–148

*See also* Abortion; Confidential health care; Mandatory reporting laws; Parental consent; Random drug testing

Thompson, Michael, 26–28

*Tinker v. Des Moines Independent Community School District,* 101, 103, 126, 132–134, 136

Title X Family Planning program, 49, 57, 71, 73–76, 78

Tweens (preteen). *See* Preteens

Twitter (online social networking site), 149

# V

Verardi, Nicole, 149–155

*Vernonia School District v. Acton,* 16, 110, 120–121, 135

Vicodin use, 106

Vietnam War protests, 132–133

*Virginia v. Black,* 133

# W

*Wall Street Journal,* 166

Weber, Kelly, 29–31

Wieber, Margi, 152

Wilson, Kerry, 92–95

Wisemore, Megan, 101–103

Wolf, James, 167

# X

Xanga (online gaming site), 152

# Y

YouGov, 146

YouTube (online video site), 23, 149